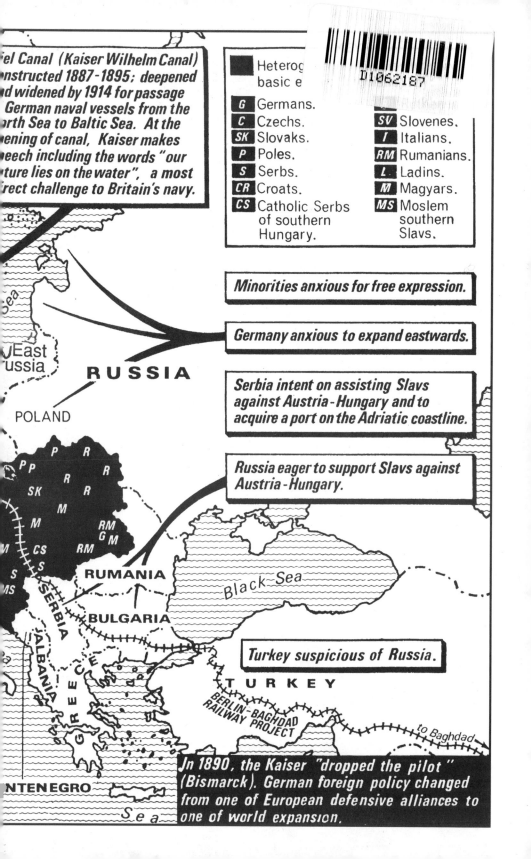

el Canal (Kaiser Wilhelm Canal) nstructed 1887-1895; deepened d widened by 1914 for passage German naval vessels from the rth Sea to Baltic Sea. At the ening of canal, Kaiser makes eech including the words "our ture lies on the water", a most rect challenge to Britain's navy.

Heterog
basic e

G Germans.
C Czechs.
SK Slovaks.
P Poles.
S Serbs.
CR Croats.
CS Catholic Serbs of southern Hungary.

SV Slovenes.
I Italians.
RM Rumanians.
L Ladins.
M Magyars.
MS Moslem southern Slavs.

Minorities anxious for free expression.

Germany anxious to expand eastwards.

Serbia intent on assisting Slavs against Austria-Hungary and to acquire a port on the Adriatic coastline.

Russia eager to support Slavs against Austria-Hungary.

Turkey suspicious of Russia.

RUSSIA

East ussia

POLAND

P P P
P R
R
SK R R
M
M RM
M
CS RM
G
M

RUMANIA

S
S
SERBIA

MS

ALBANIA

BULGARIA

Black Sea

GREECE

TURKEY

BERLIN-BAGHDAD RAILWAY PROJECT

to Baghdad

NTENEGRO

Se a

Jn 1890, the Kaiser "dropped the pilot" (Bismarck). German foreign policy changed from one of European defensive alliances to one of world expansion.

FORWARD, MARCH!

This photograph was made from a portrait of Lieutenant Ernst Rosenhainer. It was painted by G.Fr.Holle in 1915 while Lieutenant Rosenhainer was on leave in Neustrelitz, Germany. He wears the Iron Cross Second Class and the Reuss Honor Cross Third Class with Swords.

FORWARD, MARCH!

Memoirs of a German Officer

by
Lieutenant Ernst Rosenhainer
Translated and edited by Ilse R. Hance

WHITE MANE BOOKS

This White Mane Books publication
was printed by
Beidel Printing House, Inc.
63 West Burd Street
Shippensburg, PA 17257-0152 USA

In respect for the scholarship contained herein, the acid-free paper used in this book meets the guidelines for permanence and durability of the Committee on Production Guidelines for Book Longevity of the Council on Library Resources.

For a complete list of available publications
please write
White Mane Books
Division of White Mane Publishing Company, Inc.
P.O. Box 152
Shippensburg, PA 17257-0152 USA

Library of Congress Cataloging-in-Publication Data

Rosenhainer, Ernst.
     Forward march! : memoirs of a German officer / by Ernst
Rosenhainer : translated and edited by Ilse R. Hance.
        p.   cm.
     Includes index.
     ISBN 1-57249-158-2 (alk. Paper)
     1. Rosenhainer, Ernst.   2. World War, 1914-1918--Campaigns-
-Eastern Front.   3. World War, 1914-1918--Campaigns--Western Front.
4. World War, 1914-1918--Personal narratives, German.   5. Germany.
Heer Biography.   6. Soldiers--Germany Biography.   I. Title.
D550.R64   1999
940.4'14--dc21   99-16699
                                                                      CIP

Lieutenant Rosenhainer had placed this picture on the front page of his documentary journal. It shows the forest cemetery for the 96th Infantry Regiment near Ourscamp, France. The inscription on the war memorial reads: "Den gefallenen Kameraden, I.R.96." "To our comrades that died on the battlefield, I.R.96." It was sculpted by Lancer Kurth, 4th/96, and dedicated on March 4, 1916.

In memory of my father, Ernst Rosenhainer, commanding officer of various military units during World War I, and of the brave troops of his Infantry Regiment 96, from Thuringia, Germany.

Contents

Illustrations

Maps

Acknowledgments

I extend my deep gratitude to the following persons:

Ted Sacher, professional photographer, whose interest in history, especially World War I history, persuaded me to begin the awesome task of translating. Throughout my work I was able to turn to him for advice. His knowledge of the military and his keen eye helped explain the many photographs as well as maps included in this book.

My good friend, Roselinde Konrad, member of the American Translators Association and emerita of the University of California in Santa Barbara. For many months she guided my translation efforts with consummate skill, boundless enthusiasm, patience, and unqualified support. We doggedly pursued our common interest in doing justice to the author by arriving at a truthful as well as readable translation.

My daughter, Linda Ann Hance, whose interest in our German heritage led her, by way of Internet, to connect with Dr. Peter Hoffmann, director of the university library in Rostock, North Germany. My request for specific World War I military maps was forwarded speedily thanks to Dr. Hoffman via Hanno Lietz, Special Collections, to Holger Scheerschmidt, academically certified cartographer at the National Library in Berlin, through whose efforts I received and was able to incorporate into my book the military maps of the areas surrounding Lodz and Cracow as well as of East Galicia.

Arthur Banks, London cartographer, who made the maps of his *Military Atlas of the First World War* available to me and whose positive attitude regarding this publication and personal interest buoyed my spirits.

Helmut Ehrenspeck, map editor, who adapted many of the maps used in this book and assisted with some of the new maps.

Albert Arredondo, computer expert, without whose skill and loyal, cheerful support I could not have completed this project in due time.

Gertrude Platt, whose zeal at age 92, intimate knowledge of the English language and editorial skills deserve special applause. She helped fine-tune my translation!

Harold Strayer, retired English teacher. The manuscript underwent careful scrutiny under his practiced eyes, resulting in many improvements.

Harald Witzke, archivist at the Karbe-Wagner Archives, Neustrelitz, Germany, who furnished a 1914 military map of cave areas in northeastern France as well as important information regarding the picture of the Adolf-Friedrich Cave.

Robert Mc Grath, owner of the WWI Aero Bookshop in Medfield, Massachusetts, for advertising White Mane publications, including "Forward, March!".

Lieutenant Commander Sander-Nagashima and Captain Hoffmann from the Military History Research Institute in Potsdam, Germany, for responding to my requests and to Helma Burger for her very personal and dedicated assistance upon the occasion of my visit in 1998.

All friends and former colleagues whose critical reading of the manuscript contributed to a much improved text. Frau Vera Rosenhainer, Germany, for making available a photograph of her father-in-law's portrait from 1915.

Last but not least, Randy Gaulke. At the East Coast meeting of the Western Front Association in April 1997, upon learning of my translation in progress, he set the publishing process in motion by immediately contacting Dr. Martin Gordon, executive editor of the White Mane Publishing Company. I thank Dr. Gordon for laying the groundwork in the proper preparation of the manuscript, and Diane Gordon, associate editor, for her careful reading and invaluable suggestions.

Portrait of Lieutenant Ernst Rosenhainer in the Rosenhainer family dining room.

Introduction

There he was before me, my father, Ernst Rosenhainer, painted in oil, life-size, in his World War I lieutenant's uniform. His was an imposing figure on the wall of his study, at least to a child growing up in the late 1920s in our provincial town of Neustrelitz in northern Germany, once the residence of the Dukes of Mecklenburg-Strelitz. To me this portrait of my father was a symbol of times gone by. (The painting was later hung in a corner of our large dining room as shown in the photograph.)

But there was something else in the bookcase: next to *Meyer's Encyclopedia*, behind a large glass window, was this leather-bound volume my older brother Günther referred to as "Papa's *Kriegstagebuch*," Dad's wartime journal. I was not to open this important document until 60 years later (20 years after my father's death in 1970) when my half-brother, Horst, invited me to share with him our father's legacy.

It was a bittersweet experience to see my father come alive in a book he had written during and after World War I, years before I was born. According to my oldest sister, Gisela, he never really fulfilled his dream of earning a doctorate by using his completed war document as the basis for his dissertation. Illness in the family (my mother passed away in 1927) that left my father to care for three teenage children and myself, the baby in the family, may have been a factor. At any rate, my father rarely mentioned the war while I was growing up, and of course, I seldom saw him after immigrating to the United States in 1946.

But in this book he came alive: my patriarchal father, patriot, company commander, humanist, nature lover...Born in 1884, in Eisenach, Thuringia, he was surrounded by a cultural heritage that left its imprint on him: He grew up after Germany had finally become a sovereign state in 1871 and became renowned the world over for her cultural achievements in music, literature, and philosophy. The strides she had taken since the Industrial Revolution in the fields of science and technology were well recognized, and she was beginning to flex her political muscle to take her place among the major nations of Europe.

These were good and prosperous times in Germany. I remember my father recounting the first salary he received in 1908 when he had started a two-year required assistantship, teaching English and French at the "Gymnasium" in our town. "The money that I put in my pockets then were real 'Goldmarks,' and they were heavy," he once remarked with pride.

In 1910 my father volunteered for one year of military training in the Army Reserves before returning to his teaching post (and marriage!) in 1911. His military training ground was not in Neustrelitz, his new home, but in Gera, Thuringia, probably because Gera had been the city of his youth—and of his ancestors (traced back to the 13th century). Proud of his country that had achieved so much in the last century, Ernst Rosenhainer put on his lieutenant's uniform on August 5, 1914, when the Reserves were called up to serve their country and fight for "Kaiser and Reich." He was swept up in a wave of patriotic fervor not unlike that so vividly described years later in Erich Maria Remarque's book, *All Quiet on the Western Front.* Only once my father talked to me about this event and how it contrasted with the subdued feelings accompanying the soldiers' induction at the beginning of World War II, when we both saw them marching to the barracks in our garrison town. It was then that my little half-brother asked, "Papa, why is there war?"

But that question never occurred to those patriotic soldiers in 1914 who didn't doubt their country's just cause and their duty to defend its honor. This patriotism never failed my father in the weeks and months ahead of seemingly never-ending marches, battles, and trench warfare. Having been a teacher back home, he had the qualities needed to lead, first as a platoon and later as a company commander. At the same time, he was sensitive to the people and cultures he encountered, having studied foreign languages, literatures, and the humanities in general at the universities of Leipzig, Jena, and Geneva (Switzerland). In fact, during World War II he would serve as an interpreter in France.

There is no doubt that by writing his daily journal during those years at the front he would later vividly remember the more poignant encounters with local people and express his deeply felt emotions in often powerful language describing the hardships and terror of battle on the one hand and the relief and inspiration found in the natural world around him on the other.

My father, the romantic, used to take my little brother and me on long walks along our nearby lake, through the local 18th-century palace gardens and, often on Sundays, through the beautiful pine forests surrounding our town. Especially on Pentecost Sunday, he made it a point to rouse our family before dawn to experience the awakening of nature on our one-hour hike through the woods. Our reward was breakfast at a popular outdoor café while a band played happy tunes from a bandshell to celebrate the occasion. On our way home we were permitted, to our delight, to pick some of the first flowers of the season. To this day I remember those small yellow flowers.

My father's more practical nature persuaded him to purchase a plot of land, not far from his apartment house in which we lived. There he could dig and plant to his heart's content. One corner was reserved for me so that I could create my own flower garden, a hobby which carried over into my adult life. On our walks to this garden we usually passed through a working class neighborhood, with houses very modest but with flower boxes on the window sills. "Don't ever look down on poor folks," my father once said. "They often have warm and caring hearts for they know what it means to endure hardships." These were unusual words in a class-conscious society.

From his journal one might deduce that there wasn't much personal rapport between him and the enlisted men. But one has to bear in mind that during World War I the distinction between ranks was strictly and automatically maintained. This explains why officers almost always had separate quarters, and in the trenches shared their dugout only with their personal orderlies. Their free time was usually spent among other officers.

My father's own humanity was put to the test during his years on the front where he faced friend and foe alike. His journal shows that, as company commander, he was always concerned for the well-being of the troops under his command. He never questioned his duty as a soldier. On a personal level he not only respected the enemy but at times, when he was not directly involved in combat himself, "rooted" for those enemy soldiers that were struggling bravely to survive in dangerous situations. The fleeing population and innocent children were of much concern to him. Upon entering a house in a deserted village, my father noticed a Christmas tree, "...and next to it were tree decorations of gold and silver paper evidently made by the children for the approaching Christmas season. It was heartbreaking..."

Of course, the devastation caused by the battles fought on both fronts was extremely unsettling, to say the least, and left a profound impression on the soldiers. They needed a strong constitution and inner resources that would vary with each individual. To occasionally hum a tune with his fellow officers while marching forward or to be drawn into the gaiety and laughter of soldiers playacting for comic relief, were indeed uplifting experiences for my father who loved to sing and take advantage of the fine theater performances back home. Under my father's tutelage I saw my first opera, Beethoven's "Fidelio." Once I heard him exclaim (while practicing an aria himself), "Oh, why couldn't I be gifted like the Great Caruso!" Three years after my mother's death, my father married a professional singer.

My father always resisted generally held national prejudices. For instance, in regard to the "battle worthiness" of the American soldier in World War I, he conceded this: "We assumed the American soldiers, inexperienced as they were, would be no good on the battlefield, but they proved us wrong. They were brave soldiers!" (It sounds almost like a premonition, for during World War II his oldest son would fight on the side of the United States.) He was willing to listen without offering a counter-argument, as for instance in the case of the "little guy" in France who said this about the war, "This war is all the fault of the capitalists!"

It is curious to note my father's fascination with the presence of such a large Jewish population in Polish cities and villages, which he was apparently not used to in his own country. To him, the orthodox Jew, often wearing his characteristic cap (yarmulke), seemed to stand out among the local population. People, by and large, did not have the travel experience in those days that the world has today (nor could they live vicariously through the medium of television) so that seeing these strangely clad orthodox Jews, en masse, must have come as a big surprise to a German soldier. My father's reverent description of a Jewish home in prayer the night before their Sabbath sheds additional light on his experience with the Jewish population during World War I. Ironically, my Lutheran father had married into a Protestant family of Jewish descent, a fact that was to haunt him during the Nazi years when anti-Jewish laws were enacted in 1935 (the so-called "Nuremberg Laws"). As a result, three of his four children from this first marriage immigrated to the United States at different times. (One daughter died in Germany in 1942.)

Born in Eisenach, a stronghold of the Protestant faith where Martin Luther had once translated the New Testament into German, my father, too, raised his family in this Lutheran faith. But he himself was not a regular churchgoer because, as he explained to me in the 1930s, "They have transferred our best but often outspoken minister to a small community. He used to craft his sermons into a rich fabric of Biblical references and human experiences that were uplifting and spoke to our hearts. It was a joy then to attend church. Today it just isn't the same..." The only time our family would attend church together was for the Christmas and Easter holidays. Christmas at our home was an unforgettable experience with the children gathered around the tree, candles lit, my father at the piano to accompany our singing of the many best-loved Christmas carols. Small wonder that "Christmas at the front" was a recurring theme in his journal.

When World War I ended with Germany's defeat, my father did not take down his portrait of a proud officer in the German army. I sometimes wondered why not, but my feeling is that my father was proud of having fought valiantly for four long years in the Kaiser's army, proud to have fought under the leadership of the venerated Field Marshal Paul von Hindenburg, for whom he would later vote in those fateful elections of 1933. Perhaps, in his mind, he never lost the First World War, for wasn't it the Russians that had come to them to broker a peace at the Galician Front in November 1917?

However, after World War II, that shameful period in German history, my father took down the painting and crushed it with his feet. "It's no use hanging on to a symbol that no longer represents reality," he later explained to me on one of my visits to his new home in what was then West Germany.

It had obviously been difficult for him to give up the Germany he had fought for in World War I, a Germany he had loved and whose cultural treasures and humaneness he had incorporated into his own life in so many ways.

Ilse R. Hance
January 1998

Thanks to Arthur Banks' copyrighted maps I was able to include all major campaigns. His map of the Battle of Lodz (Map 9a) omitted my father's 38 Division of Mackensen's Ninth Army. This omission has been corrected by H. Ehrenspeck. Two World War I military maps, published in 1914, outline the combat areas in which my father participated. My father, undoubtedly, verified his own recollections after the war by consulting military archives that existed at the time. In some instances, I could not show the exact location of small villages my father mentioned to document the routes and areas of combat in which his own regiment had been involved. The map on page 95 I obtained from the Karbe-Wagner Archives in Neustrelitz, Germany.

Most of the pictures were placed on the same page as in my father's document. The captions are mine unless quoted from the original photos.

In my translation I retained an occasional change of tenses from the past to the present whenever possible to conform with my father's original writing.

The name "Poland" as it appears in the text or on the various World War I maps refers to "Russian Poland" since Poland was partitioned for the third (and last) time in 1795 with the middle section, the largest, incorporated into Russia. Austria annexed the southern part, i.e. "Galicia," and Germany the remaining territory west of the Warta River (Map 9a). Polish forces during World War I fought under Russian and later under Austrian and German command. Some legions joined the French army.

I have added introductory paragraphs for Chapters One, Three, and Six in order to clarify each particular situation.

Although my father refers to "Military Archives," he never explains where these may have been located. I believe that he may have found archival records either in Berlin, the capital of Germany, or in Gera, Thuringia, where he had received his military training before World War I. He does refer to the "Department of Defense" at the end of his page on "Military Decorations and Awards" (Appendix C).

I.R.H.

Chapter One

OUTBREAK OF WAR

A London Visit

My father had been teaching English and French at the "Gymnasium" (i.e., in the German secondary school system) in Neustrelitz, Germany, since 1908. In 1914 he decided to use the summer break for a "language refresher course" in England together with his old high school and college friend, Dr. W. Pietzsch. My mother remained at home to look after their two children, both under two years old. The possibility of a war in the immediate future was far from their minds.

We finally embarked upon our trip to England during a summer vacation in 1914. It was something my old high school and college friend, Dr. W. Pietzsch, and I had planned some time ago while still at the university of Jena. We left Germany around the middle of July and chose a route via Antwerp, to travel from there via Harwich to London, and later to Oxford. In searing heat we arrived in the Belgian lowlands after a long journey through German and Dutch territory. We left the train in the impressive railroad station, with its slightly eclectic architecture, in order to spend a few days in the metropolis of Belgian world trade. There we admired the magnificent cathedral and other monuments of an old and venerable architecture, visited the huge port and the area around it with warehouses of the trading companies, and saw the unsurpassed zoo with its vast and well-endowed aquarium. We heard many languages of the civilized world spoken around us, mostly French in the more well-to-do quarters, Flemish and English near the harbor. Still, one could also hear German frequently. The flourishing German school under the leadership of Professor Dr. Gaster in Antwerp is testimony to the fact that German culture and language had long ago taken root in Antwerp. We found it intriguing to research the culture of such an old city which had changed hands several times in the course of the centuries, until in 1832 it was incorporated into the Belgian state. Its foremost architect, Brialmont, was instrumental in transforming Antwerp to a fortress of great importance.

While still on the train we saw some of its fortifications which we eyed with a certain shy reverence. We asked ourselves for what purpose does Belgium, this neutral small state, need such fortifications? By chance we met a young fellow in Antwerp, whose parents were German, but who himself was a naturalized Belgian citizen and as such had served in the Belgian army. With him we discussed heatedly the current political scene, even asked ourselves on whose side Belgium would fight in case of a European war. The political horizon was clouded, to be sure.

On June 28, 1914, the Austrian successor to the throne, Franz Ferdinand, and his wife, had died at the hand of a cowardly murderer. Austria demanded from Serbia a justification and certain guarantees for the future. Serbia seemed to be disinclined to fulfill these demands. Nevertheless, everyone at first looked upon this dispute as a purely Austrian-Serbian affair and we were pretty much worry-free. Hardly anyone thought of a big war. Those in the seaside resorts seemed to enjoy their stay and relish the fruits of peaceful times. We therefore continued on our journey. One night in the harbor of Antwerp we climbed onto the steamer that was to take us to Harwich. Impressive and big, the city rose above the water. Peacefully, the ship was gliding down the River Schelde in the evening hour. A thunderstorm was brewing. Lightning and thunder took turns in quick succession. Lightning hit the harbor area and lit up the city with bright flashes. It seemed like a foreboding of what was to come. While we were going out into the world, carefree, a great storm was gathering. Soon a different kind of lightning was to emblazon the city's horizon, and the mighty German mortars were to lay to ruin its fortifications.

When we awoke the next morning, the English coastline and the Port of Harwich appeared on the horizon. By noon we were in London. The vast comings and goings of this metropolis left their indelible mark upon us. We saw London Bridge, from where we were able to watch the bustle of the harbor area, the London docks with many riches from all over the world, then the historic Tower, the venerable Westminster Abbey, St. Paul's Cathedral, etc. In Richmond we found out how the British pass their leisure hours in God's beautiful nature; in short, these were serene, peaceful hours which we experienced there, not marred by any feeling of political unrest. The only thing the British might be concerned with was their feud with the Irish and a potential civil war. And yet, an attentive observer had the distinct feeling that something was in the air.

The discussions with the Serbs continued with no results. We were only one day in Oxford, where we had planned to enroll in summer school, when the Serbian-Austrian hostilities erupted. Every few hours we rushed into town in order to buy the latest newspapers. Life in the streets continued normally. This whole affair seemed to have nothing to do with the British in the beginning. But we had become worried, for Russia intervened and had mobilized a large part of its army and had it assembled near the German-Austrian border. Faced with such ominous ventures, Germany could no longer remain neutral without exposing herself to the greatest danger. She firmly took sides with her allies.

We found ourselves in a confounded situation. We expected the British to take sides with our adversaries. What to do? Should we return to Germany at once or wait and see what would happen? In order to discuss the matter, we walked into a local restaurant and were soon surrounded by at least 25 Germans, all greatly upset, especially the women who threw up their hands, gesticulating, and denouncing roundly the attitude of the Serbs and the Russians. Most of them decided to stay; however, we preferred to depart from England the next day. To be absolutely certain we first sent a telegram home with the request to let us know whether we needed to come. When we received no answer, we returned to London. Meanwhile the situation had worsened again. The English journals reported, "Russia mobilizes" and "Germany prepares for war." We had no other choice but to proceed immediately to Folkestone, where the ship was anchored for its crossing to Vlissingen. To my great astonishment, my name was called when the train arrived and a telegram was handed to me that had been forwarded from Oxford. But the news was, "No need to come!" After some debate we decided to go after all.

The ship to Vlissingen was rather crowded; many passengers were in the same situation as we. A few ladies from London, who owned a private German school there, were on their way to the Hartz mountains for a summer vacation. What difficult situation would they get into? It was a beautiful, peaceful night voyage. Searchlights directed their bright beams onto every passing ship. Early in the morning we landed in Vlissingen. We had had little sleep and were rather fatigued. At first we didn't want to continue from Vlissingen, but instead wait for the latest news. If it was favorable, we would then do some sightseeing of the Dutch cities in order to at least put our holidays to some good use. The last reports didn't reveal much. We therefore took a leisurely walk on the

beach and admired the ocean. Other than a few children, we were probably the only ones along the beach. The hotels seemed utterly deserted.
For perhaps two hours we slept in a hotel before a certain restlessness
forced us back into town. The most recent Dutch telegrams announced
that Germany was mobilizing. Although it hadn't come to that yet, this
false alarm simply drove us to the railroad station.

It was around six o'clock in the evening and our train to Berlin left
at seven o'clock. At every railroad station we encountered large masses
of people eager to get the latest news. At the German border we heard
loud voices singing "Die Wacht am Rhein" ["The Watch on the Rhine"]
and "Gott erhalte Franz, den Kaiser" ["May God keep Franz, the Em-
peror"]. Apparently, Austrian soldiers from the reserves were leaving,
but also German soldiers, especially sailors. Bridges and tunnels were
already occupied by the military, the first warlike picture. The next morning I was in Berlin.

Chapter Two

CAMPAIGN IN THE WEST: AUGUST 1914

Call to Arms and Departure

Without any further delay I continued to Rostock via Neustrelitz [both located in northern Germany]. Emotional reunion with wife and children in my in-laws' house. War was declared on August 1. August 4 I arrived at my troop contingent in Gera (Reuss) [the Duchy of Reuss]. I was assigned as a lieutenant to the 4th Company of the 7th Thuringian Infantry Regiment, No. 96. Hostilities had already begun and we could hardly contain our impatience to get out into the field of combat. Endless columns of reserves moved through the courtyard, where they were given their uniforms. What a morale booster it was to see all these strong, healthy bodies! On August 8 we gaily left the city accompanied by the melodies of "Deutschland, Deutschland über alles" and "Die Wacht am Rhein" ["The Watch on the Rhine"]. Earlier, a solemn field service in the courtyard reminded us of the seriousness of the hour. "To win or to die" was the theme of the minister (the Reverend Thomas). The appearance of His Excellency, the Duke of Reuss, and of His Excellency, the heir apparent, invested the ceremony with special dignity. In a speech, the duke pointed out that Germany had been dragged into this war through the infamous politics of the "Entente," and now Germany's sons had to go out and fight to defend Germany's honor. Our unwavering trust in the future made parting easier. Friends and acquaintances accompanied us to the railroad station. So much hand shaking and embracing and waving good-bye! Many soldiers were to look into the faces of their loved ones for the last time. We would have to endure a long separation, perhaps forever. For the last time I saw my dear mother, whose eyes followed our departure with sadness and wistfulness. I was never to see her again. Probably the worry for her three sons on the battlefields hastened her early end (May 6, 1915).

The Battle for Namur

Yet, at the time, our upbeat state of mind would not be subdued by sad and serious thoughts. Before long we were seated in the train. The question "Where are we going?" was on everybody's mind. From the direction the train was taking we were soon able to guess. We were going west by way of Weimar-Eisenach-Cassel-Marburg. The landscape was bathed in glittering sunlight. A last farewell we bid you, spruce and fir of the Altenburg land! Once more we look upon the city of Goethe [Weimar]; the golden cross of the Wartburg [in Eisenach] is gleaming in the last rays of the sun. How tranquil, how peaceful is the countryside! And war looms on the horizon? It is simply unthinkable. And yet, this land must not be trampled on by hostile forces; these peaceful towns and villages must not go up in flames. Already our troops are on enemy territory; one big fortress has already been conquered. The waves of joyful tumult surrounding us during the entire train journey knew no end. They seemed literally to carry us into enemy territory. At every train stop, friendly and willing hands offered us refreshments, and when the train pulled out we were accompanied by warm good-byes—Auf Wiedersehn! And a thousand hands were waving until the train rounded the next corner. How deeply we were moved when we crossed the Rhine River near Cologne. Was there any other way of greeting it than with the famous battle hymn, "Es braust ein Ruf wie Donnerhall" ["Our shout rises high like thunder's echo"]. This time the song took on a meaning quite different from that of celebrations of the Battle of Sedan [on September 1, 1870, a decisive victory by German forces in the Franco-Prussian War]. This time we were ready to act on our oath and, spilling our blood, do battle as our fathers had in 1870/71. The enemy was never going to cross our River Rhine. In the shadows of the darkening night the broad ribbon of the river glittered below us.

Another day of traveling and we were near the Belgian border (Map 1). In St. Vith we got off and immediately set out on our march under a deep blue August sky. The hot, blistering sun made our march across the mountains quite an ordeal. A number of our men dropped from exhaustion, especially since many of the reservists were no longer accustomed to such long marches. When we reached the border control, we were greeted with a friendly "hello" by our customs officers before crossing the Belgian border with shouts of "hurrah!" Right away we came upon the Belgians' first preparations for war. Huge trees had been cut down and placed across the road to block the forward march of the German troops. However, the Belgians were out of luck, for we forced them

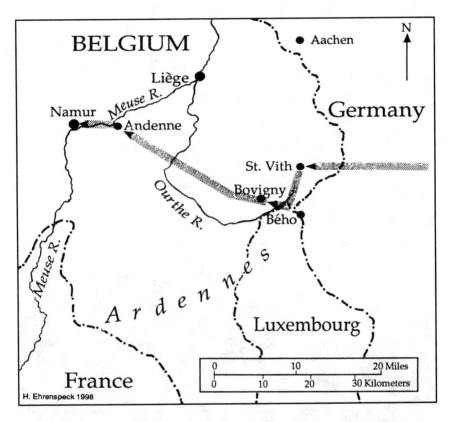

Map 1

Belgium

By August 13, 1914, Lt. R.'s company, part of Regiment No. 96, was well on its way toward the fortress of Namur.

to remove the logs from the road with their own hands. Thus we reached the first Belgian village Bého (in German = Buchholz) without any further obstacles. Here we were intrigued by the first French signs. We stayed in cramped quarters until August 13. The people in the village were afraid and rather subdued. Our quarters were extremely modest, and our daily routine was much like a regular maneuver. Once in a while our sentries would start shooting, then stop. As for the rest, everything remained quiet and there was no sign of the enemy.

Early on August 13 we left. We were put in charge of railroad protection. Our 4th Company was the outpost in Bovigny. We were stationed on a farm where we were getting milk, bread, and other foods. The people were friendly and moreover knew German. I had breakfast under shade trees, then poured a whole bucket of water over my body to refresh myself. But soon we had to move on and secure the railroad line Cicereux-Bovigny. This area resembled Thuringia. Between the mountains were picturesque valleys filled with rushing mountain streams where we'd go in for a swim every day, which we thoroughly enjoyed after our exhausting marches on dusty roads. Often we marched past castles surrounded

Third from left, Lieutenant Rosenhainer (Lt. R.) with fellow officers while quartered in Ottré, Belgium, on August 15, 1914. Their names, written on the reverse side of photo, are, *from right:* Kirschmann, First Lieutenant von der Becke, First Lieutenant Schweizer, Second Lieutenant Ebers, Second Lieutenant Meysenburg, Second Lieutenant Rosenhainer, Seond Lieutenant Kaye, and, *seated in front,* Second Lieutenant Grimmer.

by beautiful green parks. On August 14 we quartered in the lovely castle of Provedroux, high up on a steep mountain. However, there were no friendly hosts to welcome us. The occupants had fled; all the furniture was gone. But at least we had spacious rooms at our disposal. Even our beds of straw were welcome. Seemingly without a care in the world, we had a cup of coffee in the park under age-old trees, and in the evening a bottle of wine. We enjoyed a fantastic view across the mountains and refreshed ourselves with a swim in the park's pond. It was too bad that the fruit on the trees wasn't ripe yet, but in a nursery juicy grapes were already ripening under glass. Our supply train and the field kitchen were on hand in the picturesque courtyard in front of the castle. But our fairy tale life in the castle didn't last long. Our idyllic rest was suddenly interrupted by marching orders around noon on August 15.

After a very strenuous march we found quarters in Ottré. In their cemetery we buried the first soldier from the 94th Regiment. He had suffered a heat stroke. We then came to Hothon on the Ourthe River, a small town in a romantic setting. Here we were able to buy some food, cigars, and other items. We came closer and closer to the Maas River [Meuse]. There had been heavy fighting already near Dinan, and we knew that—after Lüttich [Liège]—the Maas fortress of Namur was under siege. That's where we were going. On August 19 we quartered once again in Habine, which we reached under a searing sun. As yet we did not have the impression that we were in enemy territory, especially since the people there were very friendly and obliging.

On August 20 we moved on early in the morning, around four o'clock. Gradually we closed in on the city of Namur. For the first time in this world war we received orders to attack. That really gave us a jolt! We were faced with something completely new and unknown. What will it be like? "The brigade is to take possession of the hills east of Namur," was the command. We came to the edge of a forest where we were protected and from where we were able to take a good look at the area before us. Far away on the horizon we saw for the first time shells hitting one of the forts of Namur, surrounding it with big clouds of smoke. In columns we were marching down into the valley, nerves taut from excitement in expectation of what lay ahead. From below we heard weak rifle fire. We came through a village, then climbed up a hillside after navigating through a canyonlike valley. We were to clear the enemy from the hills, but the enemy was nowhere in sight. He had already withdrawn to be closer to the fortress.

We now cleared the underbrush from the young forest to make room for ourselves, leaving only the front row of trees as cover. There we stayed during the night from 21/22 August, 1914. I was sitting on a tree stump freezing in my cape and trying hard to fight an overwhelming fatigue. From the valley below I heard heavy infantry fire cracking intermittently, apparently coming from patrols. In these mountains the noise echoed loudly, as if a whole brigade were fighting. Other than that nothing much happened, and the next evening we had to leave our good position where we had hoped to stay for a while. The whole battalion gathered in a nice little village, the field kitchen arrived, and we had a large meal to prepare for the long night march ahead.

All through the night we marched to the north of the city. It was a march that taxed our endurance. Even though our legs were getting weak and wobbly and we could barely keep our eyes open, we had to keep moving. I literally fell asleep while marching, my consciousness being dimmed, to say the least. It was a rude awakening each time we stopped suddenly and one's head bumped into the mess kit of the soldier ahead. After marching through deeply carved valleys, toward morning we came to open fields near St. Berge. It had been a cold night so that it was a relief to finally watch the sun rise gloriously and to feel its quickening warmth revive our frozen limbs. It was easier now to keep our eyes open. Our cavalry division passed us riding proudly on their swift horses. After a brief halt our 4th Company was asked to leave the battalion in order to cover the supply train. Wagon after wagon rumbled down a dusty country road, with us always marching alongside. Since the wagons were moving fast at times, then again in a slow tempo, we had to adjust our steps accordingly so that the march on a dusty road under a blazing sun became all the more exhausting. We finally reached an area around noon where fighting had occurred. Houses gutted by fire told the tale. For the first time we were face to face with the misery of war.

At last we saw the beautiful valley of the Maas River before us. Below, the river meandered through the valley, and we saw one village after another. To the left of the road was a German gun firing without pause. It was at the same time subjected to volleys from the other side. Now and then we could hear the cracking sounds of infantry shooting from the woods across from us, but we weren't quite sure from whose side they were. Perhaps they came from *franc-tireurs* [snipers]? At one point when the shooting happened very close to us, I decided to check this out, but soon discovered that German soldiers were engaged in a harmless practice session, using handguns.

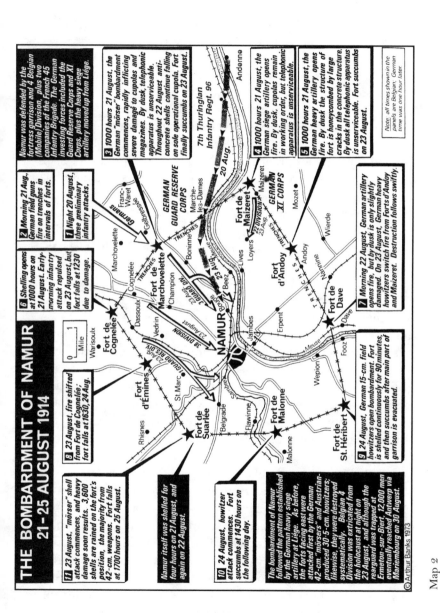

THE BOMBARDMENT OF NAMUR
21–25 AUGUST 1914

1 Night 20 August, three preliminary infantry attacks.

2 Morning 21 Aug., German field guns fire on trenches in intervals of forts.

3 1000 hours 21 August, the German "mörser" bombardment commences, rapidly inflicting severe damage to cupolas and magazines. By dusk, telephonic apparatus is unserviceable. Throughout 22 August, concrete shells continue falling on sole operational cupola. Fort finally succumbs on 23 August.

4 1000 hours 21 August, the German siege artillery opens fire. By dusk, cupolas remain in working order, but telephonic apparatus is unserviceable.

5 1000 hours 21 August, the German heavy artillery opens fire. By dusk the structure of fort is honeycombed by large cracks in the concrete structure. By dusk all telephonic apparatus is unserviceable. Fort succumbs on 23 August.

6 Shelling opens at 1000 hours on 21 August. Early-morning infantry attack repulsed on 23 August, but fort falls at 1230 due to damage.

7 Morning 22 August, German artillery opens fire, but by dusk is only slightly damaged. On 23 August, German heavy howitzers switch fire from Forts d'Andoy and Maizeret. Destruction follows swiftly.

8 23 August, fire shifted from Fort de Cognelée; fort falls at 1630, 24 Aug.

9 24 August, German 15-cm. field howitzers open bombardment. Fort is shelled continuously for 90 minutes, and then succumbs after main part of garrison is evacuated.

10 24 August, howitzer attack commences at 1430 hours on the following day.

11 23 August, "mörser" shell attack commences, and heavy damage soon results. 3,600 shells are rained on the fort's position, the majority from 42-cm. weapons. Fort falls at 1700 hours on 25 August.

Namur was defended by the fortress garrison and 4 Belgian (Mobile) Division, plus two companies of the French 45 Infantry Brigade. The German investing forces included the Guard Reserve Corps and XI Corps, plus the heavy siege artillery moved up from Liège.

Namur itself was shelled for four hours on 21 August, and again on 22 August.

The bombardment of Namur followed the pattern established by the German heavy siege artillery at Liège. As before, the forts facing east were attacked first by the German 42-cm "mörsers" and Austrian-produced 30.5-cm. howitzers; likewise, they were destroyed systematically. Belgian 4 Division was extricated from the holocaust at night on 23 August, and although the rearguard was trapped at Ermeton-sur-Biert, 12,000 men eventually reached Antwerp via Mariembourg on 30 August.

Note: all times shown in the panels are Belgian. German time was one hour later.

7th Thuringian Infantry Regt. 96

GERMAN GUARD RESERVE CORPS

GERMAN XI CORPS

© Arthur Banks 1973

Map 2

The Bombardment of Namur: August 21–25, 1914

Regiment 96 approached the city of Namur from the east on August 20, 1914.

In Andenne we crossed the Maas River [Map 2]. The streets of the town all showed the results of very heavy fighting. There was hardly a house where the windows had not been smashed by rifle fire, and on the walls were deep holes from infantry bullets. The bridges across the Maas had been blown up, but had already been replaced by our engineers. Beyond the river we saw the city literally reduced to rubble and ashes and still burning in some places. The people squatted in front of their homes, discouraged. When the supply vehicles had left Andenne, we were all subjected to fire from one of the hills. "Herr Leutnant, rifles to the front!" was the command. I hurried up the hill with a few men and found six civilians behind a hedge, apparently working class people. An old man had been wounded by our fire, and the younger men stood around him, beseeching us, *"Vous avez un médecin, monsieur. Vous êtes bon, laissez-nous libres, monsieur, nous ne sommes pas coupables, nous n'avons pas d'armes."* ["You have a doctor, sir. You are a good man, let us go free, sir, we are not guilty, we have no weapons."] I could not find out whether they had been shooting; however, I could not find any weapons. I therefore sent these men to the guard post in Andenne and hurried on with my men to locate my company. Late that night, I caught up with them again, having exchanged friendly greetings with our comrades, the military escorts of the Austrian motorized units. Since the regiment had obviously moved on in quite a different direction, our company started out on its own (the third night without sleep) until we finally managed to get some sleep around 2 a.m., dropping dead tired in a ditch along the road to seek shelter from the cold. The strenuous marches of the last few days and nights had been tremendous. At dawn we marched on in the direction of the loudest artillery and rifle fire and where at times we heard confused shouts of hurrah by German soldiers.

When daylight broke we reached the range of fire from one of the forts of Namur. One soldier in our company was wounded, our first in this war. When we finally reached a lovely, low-lying meadow we ran into the III Battalion's Infantry-Regiment 71 and joined them. At this point we were starved and longed for a cup of coffee. The field kitchen's arrival was greeted enthusiastically, and we felt refreshed and alive again after our hot morning coffee. We lay down in the grass happy to have finally found a regiment which we could join. The free time was used by our kitchen crew to chase down the well-fed cattle in the meadow. It was a funny sight as the cattle would scamper away again and again, leaving the kitchen crew without a successful catch. In the end, though, the crew's efforts were rewarded, and soon there was meat in the kettle, cooking away!

Sudden marching orders sent us on our way again. It was August 23. Heavy artillery opened a hellish fire, the shells whizzed through the air hissing and roaring, then hit their target with a thud. All around town, houses were burning. Now and then we saw a few wounded. And suddenly—what a beautiful sight! Our flags were proudly flying ahead. There was no stopping us; off we went, officers first, some still on horseback. Then we rushed through hedges and over fences. We cut through the entanglements, went down a railroad embankment. Here and there lay a dead Belgian. When we heard the cracking of rifles, we deployed into skirmishing order. Before us were already many lines in open formation. Over there by the forest we could see shrapnel bursting now and then. The sheaves of corn were still in the fields. Soon we were hit by stronger machine gun and rifle fire. Now we jumped from one stack of sheaves to another. Fortunately for us the Belgians aimed mostly too high and the bullets whizzed above our heads with a hissing sound. Encouraged, we lifted our heads slowly and saw the Belgians turn and run toward a wooded area from which they hoped to escape. We advanced slowly until we finally came upon the enemy's trenches that were protected by a wide net of carefully laid-out wire barricades. Curious, we took a good look at these installations when, lo and behold, our eyes discovered what we needed most: large amounts of bread! And thus, we were bombarded with crisp loaves of bread instead of hostile bullets. Bread was thrown rapidly from the trenches by our corporals. Chewing on pieces of bread, we moved up a hill where a large number of troops had massed in front of the city gate, and higher up on the mountain we finally reached the first houses of a suburb of Namur, small houses surrounded by gardens that sloped in a rather steep decline toward the valley. A tall church building completed the picture before us. We stood there on this narrow street for a long time. I guess the march of the troops into the city had to be organized. After what our troops had experienced in Belgium earlier, safety regulations had to be put in place, for no one knew who might be hiding between the houses. It was an eerie feeling!

And before we knew it, bullets came flying from attics and other hiding places, so that, sadly, a number of officers and troops fell victim to the attack. The punishment, however, was swift: doors and windows were smashed in with a thunderous noise and soon houses suspected of being enemy hideouts went up in flames, their heat and smoke felt uncomfortably by us in these narrow streets. Screaming women and young girls spilled into their garden from a back door. It was heartrending to hear a woman beg a higher ranking officer, *"Monsieur, protégez-nous!"* ["Sir, protect us!"] One soldier, black from the smoke and half dead, stumbled out of the house and fell to the ground. In short, there was a tremendous noise and complete pandemonium all around us, heightened by the fire from the German cannon emplacements on the mountain top. After we had marched to the church on the hilltop, we placed our rifles in one area and sat down on the walls surrounding the church yard. About 50 meters before us, the field guns were shooting at the Belgians and French who were fleeing across the plains of the Maas River below. We watched from our perch as they were seeking shelter from the bursting shells behind houses, in ditches, etc. And far below we saw German troops, who apparently had prisoners with them, trying to alert our artillery to the fact that they were Germans by waving black-white-red flags. The city of Namur was ours, even if a few forts were still in the hands of the opponent. On August 25 they, too, capitulated. The battle of Namur ended in a German victory, although not a victory that would decide the campaign.

In high spirits we marched down into the city. The people were composed but very fearful, even offering us gifts as we were marching past. We stayed only one night in Namur, in fine quarters in a house vacated by its inhabitants. We were just having the noon meal we had managed to put together when the alarm signal sounded and we were told to move on immediately. All major thoroughfares were crowded with troops and soon so congested that we weren't able to leave the outskirts of the city until the onset of dusk. We had barely reached the last houses when ferocious machine gun fire rained down on us just as it had hit us when we had first entered the city. But since it was poorly aimed and in the darkness we were able to duck in the ditches by the side of the road, we sustained no losses. We didn't arrive in our overnight quarters until after midnight (between the two forts Mabonne and St. Héribert in the line of defense that was put in place around the fort). Very early the next morning we moved on. The right wing of our army (the 3rd) marched as quickly as possible in a western direction.

The Situation on the Front in Late August 1914

As far as good luck in the war was concerned, the scales had tilted to the German side. Relentlessly Germany's army drove the British and French back, and the first German cavalry was within the perimeter of Paris. From all sides reports came in of "Victorious Battles," of the "Enemy Beating Hasty Retreats," of "Decisive Victories," causing the generals of the Supreme Headquarters to believe erroneously that the final phase of the war on the Western Front had been completed, and that the time had come to regroup the troops to the Eastern Front, according to plan. From East Prussia had come disturbing news concerning the 8th

Army. Supreme Commander, General Helmuth von Moltke, had planned to send the VI Corps to the eastern theater of war. As a first step he gave orders to move our 11th Company, available after Namur, and the guard reserve corps as well as the cavalry division. It soon turned out to be a tragic mistake since their forces would have been of utmost importance on the right flank. It was the beginning of the Battle of the Marne when on September 6, 1914, the fighting started on the entire vast front between Paris and Verdun, a battle which was to decide the fate of Europe, comparable to the battles of Leipzig and Waterloo.

It was totally unexpected and came as a complete surprise when we received orders to leave immediately for the Eastern Front. We had been filled with visions of glory and the fervent desire to win this war, and we were eager to fight for victory under strong leadership, even if this meant rough times ahead and losing lives. There was no question that these sudden marching orders to the east would weigh on us heavily and tear the veil of our illusions.

Before the marching orders reached us, we had stopped for a rest in a field near Florennes, thinking that we would soon move on westward. It was an enjoyable short period of relaxation. Our men were in a happy, almost playful, mood. They organized a parade for fun. One musketeer straddled another simulating a general on horseback who was reviewing his troops. We were joking and having a good time. Only from far away one could hear the cannons roar. Still, orders for us to move into battle weren't coming. As time passed and nothing happened, our good mood evaporated. We had the strange feeling that something was amiss. That was when we were notified of the intent to move our troops east. Not a sound could be heard in the field. Those of us who had had dreams of a triumphant march into Paris were now thinking of ice-cold winters in Russia. Summer was fading fast. What would be our fate in Russia, we wondered, now that winter was almost upon us?

Chapter Three

CAMPAIGN AGAINST RUSSIA (8TH ARMY, EAST) 1914:
BATTLE OF THE MASURIAN LAKES
AND PUSH TO THE EAST

Germany's plans to quickly defeat France in the west, then move against Russia in the east were pre-empted in part by a rapid Russian attack. On August 17 Russia's 1st Army under General Pavel K. Rennenkampf launched a successful offensive against East-Prussia from the east, followed three days later by an attack by Alexander V. Samsonov's 2nd Army, moving against East-Prussia from the south (See "Plan A" on Map 3).

The new German command for the Eastern Front—a partnership between General Erich Ludendorff and General Paul von Hindenburg—decided to concentrate their forces against Samsonov's army. This led to a total defeat of the Russian 2nd Army at Tannenberg (August 26–31, Map 4). As a result, General Samsonov took his own life.

More German troops were rushed in from the Western Front to drive the rest of the Russian forces under General Rennenkampf out of East-Prussia. This battle was centered around the Masurian Lakes (Maps 4 and 5). Germany's war on two fronts had begun.

Two Great Armies Face Each Other

On September 1, 1914, we left St. Vith from where we had only a short time ago ventured into enemy territory [on the Western Front] and the train took us via Berlin-Thorn to Allenstein in East Prussia [Map 4]. As we passed Spandau on September 2, church bells were ringing to announce a big victory celebration because Field Marshal Paul von Hindenburg had defeated the Russians in another Cannae [where Hannibal had defeated the Romans in 216 B.C.] near Tannenberg, East Prussia. Soon we, too, would be standing on this huge battlefield to finish the

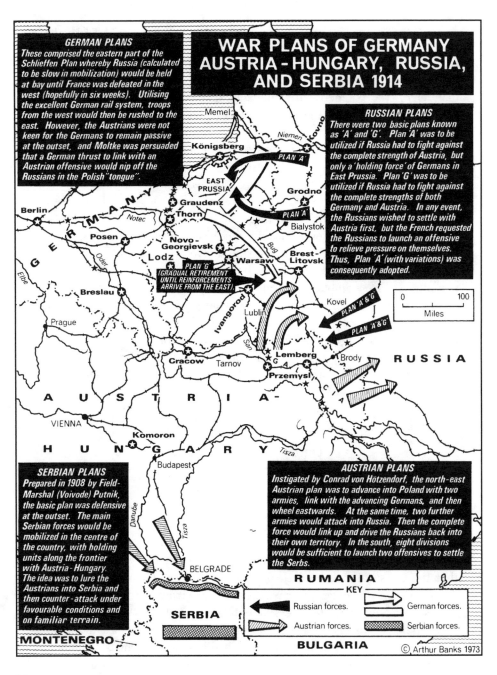

WAR PLANS OF GERMANY AUSTRIA - HUNGARY, RUSSIA, AND SERBIA 1914

GERMAN PLANS

These comprised the eastern part of the Schlieffen Plan whereby Russia (calculated to be slow in mobilization) would be held at bay until France was defeated in the west (hopefully in six weeks). Utilising the excellent German rail system, troops from the west would then be rushed to the east. However, the Austrians were not keen for the Germans to remain passive at the outset, and Moltke was persuaded that a German thrust to link with an Austrian offensive would nip off the Russians in the Polish "tongue".

RUSSIAN PLANS

There were two basic plans known as 'A' and 'G'. Plan 'A' was to be utilized if Russia had to fight against the complete strength of Austria, but only a 'holding force' of Germans in East Prussia. Plan 'G' was to be utilized if Russia had to fight against the complete strengths of both Germany and Austria. In any event, the Russians wished to settle with Austria first, but the French requested the Russians to launch an offensive to relieve pressure on themselves. Thus, Plan 'A' (with variations) was consequently adopted.

SERBIAN PLANS

Prepared in 1908 by Field-Marshal (Voivode) Putnik, the basic plan was defensive at the outset. The main Serbian forces would be mobilized in the centre of the country, with holding units along the frontier with Austria-Hungary. The idea was to lure the Austrians into Serbia and then counter-attack under favourable conditions and on familiar terrain.

AUSTRIAN PLANS

Instigated by Conrad von Hötzendorf, the north-east Austrian plan was to advance into Poland with two armies, link with the advancing Germans, and then wheel eastwards. At the same time, two further armies would attack into Russia. Then the complete force would link up and drive the Russians back into their own territory. In the south, eight divisions would be sufficient to launch two offensives to settle the Serbs.

PLAN 'A'

PLAN 'A'

PLAN 'G' (GRADUAL RETIREMENT UNTIL REINFORCEMENTS ARRIVE FROM THE EAST).

PLAN 'A & G'

PLAN 'A & G'

0   100
Miles

KEY

Russian forces.   German forces.

Austrian forces.   Serbian forces.

© Arthur Banks 1973

Memel · Königsberg · Niemen · Kovno · EAST PRUSSIA · Graudenz · Thorn · Grodno · Berlin · Notec · Posen · Novo-Georgievsk · Bialystok · Breslau · Lodz · Warsaw · Brest-Litovsk · Prague · Ivangorod · Lublin · Kovel · Cracow · Tarnov · Lemberg · Przemysl · Brody · RUSSIA · VIENNA · Komoron · HUNGARY · Tisza · Budapest · Danube · BELGRADE · RUMANIA · SERBIA · MONTENEGRO · BULGARIA · Odra · Elbe · San · Bug · GERMANY · AUSTRIA-

Map 3

War Plans of Germany, Austria-Hungary, Russia, and Serbia, 1914

In 1914 and early 1915 Lt. R. was engaged in battle in East Prussia, then east of Cracow and in the area surrounding Lodz. He fought on the Russian Front in East Galicia in 1916 and 1917.

work begun by our great field marshal. When the Russians had lost the battle near Tannenberg and General Pavel K. Rennenkampf, the commander of the Njemen army that had spread out between Deime and Angerapp, got word of the collapse of Alexander V. Samsonov's army, he established a front line from Labian via Nordenburg to Angerburg, thereby creating a firm barrier from the Courian Lagoon to the big Masurian Lakes. In addition, Russian troops from around Grodno were put in place on one flank near Lyck. Rennenkampf decided to fight defensively.

The tumult of battle in the woods and near the lakes of Tannenberg had subsided. And while the huge booty of war was gathered up, Hindenburg's airmen were already flying east, surveying the freshly dug encampments of Rennenkampf's Njemen army. A different kind of field marshal might have granted his exhausted troops some much-deserved rest after their enormous exertions near Tannenberg. And he might have been satisfied to merely push the Russians out of East Prussia. But Hindenburg wanted more. He wanted to get Rennenkampf into another Cannae by attacking his entire flank and thus dealing him a deadly blow. As early as September 4, 1914, Hindenburg had his 8th Army move in an eastern direction, from the cities of Ortelsburg-Bischofsburg-Heilsberg-Mehlsack. It was re-enforced by our XI Corps recruited from the Western Front, the guard-reserve corps, and the 8th Cavalry Division that had fought only a few days ago in the Belgian Ardennes.

On the Cossacks' Trail

Our regiment started marching from Allenstein [Map 4]. We belonged to the advance guard, under the command of Major General Freiherr von Manstein. By September 5, we were positioned in Seeburg, and on the evening of September 6, our company took over the outpost near Plössen. It was reported that Cossacks were nearby, but so far there was no sign of the enemy. Not until the next day did we find evidence that the Cossacks had been through the area near Gross-Wolfsdorf. In deserted enemy bivouacs there was still lots of straw lying around, canned goods, bottles of wine, leftovers of butchered cattle, feathers of chickens that had been consumed. The civilians had fled; there wasn't a soul around; every house had been broken into, and inside was total chaos. Outside in the yards there were individual pieces of beautiful furniture. Many buildings, especially the inns and the railroad stations, were gutted except for the walls. We continued on our strenuous march through the vast plains. Most villages were ravaged and vacated.

On September 8 we came upon the Russians. Our cavalry patrols had already been engaged in serious skirmishes. Now it was our turn.

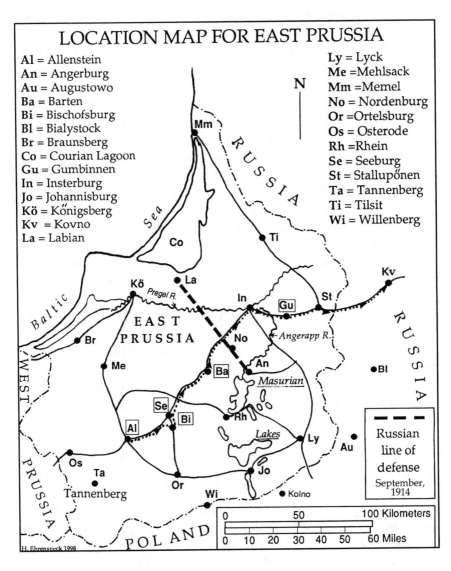

LOCATION MAP FOR EAST PRUSSIA

Al = Allenstein
An = Angerburg
Au = Augustowo
Ba = Barten
Bi = Bischofsburg
Bl = Bialystock
Br = Braunsberg
Co = Courian Lagoon
Gu = Gumbinnen
In = Insterburg
Jo = Johannisburg
Kö = Königsberg
Kv = Kovno
La = Labian

N

Ly = Lyck
Me =Mehlsack
Mm =Memel
No = Nordenburg
Or =Ortelsburg
Os = Osterode
Rh =Rhein
Se = Seeburg
St = Stallupönen
Ta = Tannenberg
Ti = Tilsit
Wi = Willenberg

RUSSIA

Sea

Mm

Co

Ti

Baltic

Kö   Pregel R.   La   In   Gu   St   Kv

EAST
PRUSSIA   No   Angerapp R.   RUSSIA

Br   Me   Ba   An   Bl

Masurian

Se   Bi   Rh

Al   Lakes   Ly

Os   Au

Ta   Or   Jo

Tannenberg   Wi   Kolno

- - -
Russian
line of
defense
September,
1914

0	50	100 Kilometers

| 0 | 10 | 20 | 30 | 40 | 50 | 60 Miles |

POLAND

H. Ehrensbeck 1998

Map 4

Location Map for East Prussia

Lt. R. and his regiment moved northeast against the Russian line of defense between Labian and Angerburg.

From now on we stayed only in makeshift quarters. On September 8, around nine o'clock in the morning, we set out from Gross-Wolfsdorf. Our 4th Company (4th Company Commander First Lieutenant von der Becke) began its forward march toward Barten via Freudenberg. It was a beautiful, late-summer morning, a bit nippy, but there was still bright sunshine warming us from a clear blue sky. And so we were in an upbeat mood as we marched toward the enemy. Since we were part of the forefront, an encounter with the enemy was possible at any time. The most advanced group proceeded carefully in open formation. At 8:45 a.m. the 1st Battalion received orders to march through the so-called *Grosse Gans* [Big Goose]. Thus we were forced to separate from our company and to march on alone, a forlorn little troop! It was a swampy terrain, crisscrossed by larger wooded areas and small hills.

At first we crossed a big forest. Our company commander, von der Becke, moved ahead along the western edge of the forest with a small contingent. As the platoon commander, I was to follow straight through the woods with the rest of the company. It was difficult to orient ourselves since we had no maps, so we were forced to simply walk in a general direction. I had two platoons advance in skirmishing order while I proceeded with the entire third one through the dense forest. Then there were more swampy meadows. With every step we sank deeper into the morass, and once while jumping across a ditch, I found myself stuck in the brackish moor to my hips, so that my good riflemen had trouble getting me out of this soggy dilemma. After that, the forest once again closed in on us. In the end we lost contact with the front section of our platoon, and there I was, all alone with a handful of men. Our shouting and whistling was of no use — no response. Then all of a sudden nerve-wracking rifle fire crackling! By 9:30 our front line of skirmishers, facing the village of Schätzels, was bombarded with heavy fire. The shooting pointed us in the right direction.

We jumped ahead and came to an open meadow. Sssssst! Sharp hissing sounds in the air, and rifle bullets were streaking past our ears. Back into the woods—quick—and then, carefully, along the edge of the forest, behind the trees. Soon we could see our comrades firing from an embankment by the village and we jumped toward them meter by meter. (In the meantime, our artillery had started its attack.) There was no visible sign of the enemy. They were shooting at us from behind trees and bushes. Undoubtedly, these were only weak front units, which were retreating from stronger enemy forces in the direction of Assanen. Having lost one man dead and several wounded, our company marched into the village of

Schätzelshöfchen and dug in against possible enemy attacks. But we didn't stay there long. Our pilots had discovered the positions of the enemy and we now marched toward them. It was still broad daylight when we reached our own artillery position. The batteries stood there, one next to the other, silent and threatening, no sign of life and motion in evidence. Just as we reached a few barns, a terrible crash, and the first enemy shell landed close by.

Down we go! Boom, boom! There comes the second, then the third. We burrow our heads into the dirt. Everywhere black fountains of mud blast into the air, understandably putting our men on edge. In broad daylight we are an easy target for the Russians. The 3rd Company (Colonel Pfannstiehl) disperses in all directions. Like drunkards the riflemen, with their heavy backpacks, are weaving back and forth in the stubble fields, and there is danger that the leader may lose control. This goes on until they are finally able to escape into the forest, out of view of the enemy. But this "warm" reception upsets us a bit. All around our 4th Company another barrage of gunfire erupts. Our company commander shouts, "Company, get down!" Row upon row we lie there in the deep rut of the dirt road and press our bodies firmly to the ground. We lie like this for about two hours until it gets dark and the enemy can no longer see us. For the first time we really dig in (south of Henriettenfelde), a task we are not at all accustomed to and for which we are hardly prepared.

The next morning, on September 9 around 9 a.m., our artillery began shooting. The enemy returned the fire with huge volleys. We now moved forward and were positioned right behind our firing artillery in a protected basin. We lay there from eight o'clock till four in the afternoon, during which time Russian shells hit the ground only a few hundred meters away. A hot September sun glared down on us, and after the sleepless night we were overcome by irresistible fatigue. Most of us dropped down with our heads in the sand and slept soundly until evening, despite the thundering cannons and bursting shells. When we got up, one man didn't: a shell fragment had killed him. We then returned to our trenches, crouching and holding on to each other, desperately trying to get some sleep.

Strategies in East Prussia, after Tannenberg [Map 5]

Rennenkampf, whose brilliant career had soared during the Russo-Japanese War in East Asia, apparently could not reach a final strategic decision. He stopped in his tracks with his 20 infantry divisions. Whatever his plans might have been, with his vast reserves he could have easily muddied the waters for us. Hindenburg had at his disposal five corps, the

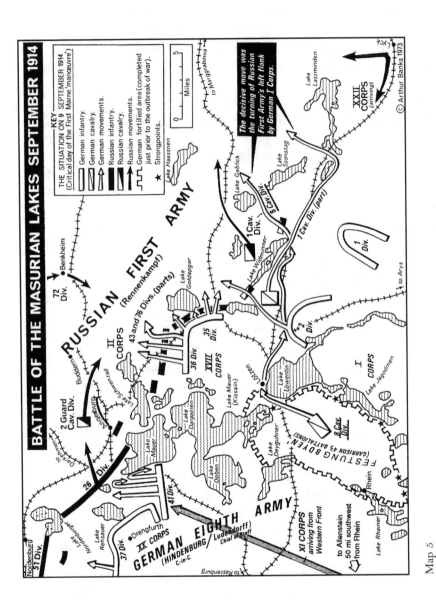

Map 5

Battle of the Masurian Lakes, September 1914

Lt. R. belonged to the XI Corps and was part of the re-enforcements from the Western Front, joining Hindenburg's 8th Army. His regiment started out in Allenstein on September 4, moving steadily northeast.

3rd Reserve Division, the Landwehr Division v.d. Goltz, two cavalry divisions. Facing him were six corps, two rifle brigades, six reserve divisions and the guard cavalry corps. With his relatively weak force, Hindenburg built up a broad front from Willenberg to Königsberg. Our XI Corps, with the XX Corps, the 1st Reserve Corps, and the guard-reserve corps had advanced against the Angerburg-Deime positions, that is, against the enemy front. Two corps were to penetrate the lake area. The 3rd Reserve Division was to march south around the Masurian Lakes followed by two cavalry divisions. This was the situation on September 6 and 7, 1914.

On September 8, the battle is raging on the entire front. Our brave troops break through the enemy's fortified positions around the lakes and continue in a northeastern direction. At this point our cavalry seems to have smooth sailing in the same direction. On September 9, the battle continues to rage on the front line between Angerburg [Map 4] and the "Kurische Haff" [Couric Lagoon]. Rennenkampf now employs massive forces against us. Near Insterburg our pilots see two Russian corps advancing and near Tilsit a third corps. Yet, Hindenburg seems not overly concerned about the middle front, even though it is rather weak. Should the Russian field marshal be successful, Hindenburg will regain control through a strong continuing attack on both flanks. On the evening of September 9, he goes so far as to wish that Rennenkampf will attack if only to score points. But Rennenkampf does not come through.

On September 10, 1914, after a sleepless night in a crouched position in our trench, I crawled out stiff as a board. It was early dawn; I was alone and sat down on the edge of the trench. Around me everything was quiet and peaceful. The forest was quite still in the morning fog. Birds started to warble their songs when suddenly I saw a figure emerging from the mist. I recognized our brigade commandant, General von Manstein. He seemed rather agitated and called out to me, "The Russians have withdrawn, too bad, too bad."

In Pursuit of the Russian Army

Without knowledge of the overall strategic battle plans, I was unable to appreciate the significance of these words at the time. In any case, Rennenkampf tried to escape a potential trap by retreating as quickly as possible and continued to withdraw. From the tracks his columns left behind we soon concluded that his army was headed toward Russia in dense triple columns while our flanks pushed sharply northeast in order to cut off his drive on Kovno [Map 4].

We, too, move forward as quickly as possible. In forced marches we cross Russian fortified zones, moving through villages that are completely gutted except for foundations and tall chimneys, until we finally catch up with the enemy again. Our batteries roll along the roads with thundering noise, disappear in hilly terrain from where shells burst forth howling and churning, then crash into the retreating Russian troops. We see Russian soldiers emerge from the gun smoke trying to escape the danger zone. The artillery moves forward with the usual noise, and the game starts all over again. Nordenburg is in sight with its big lake in which pieces of shrapnel create wide circles. Soon the city is behind us and we come to a deep basin where we can finally take a break after a strenuous march. On top of a knoll we notice our artillery taking position. Our company commander makes sure that our own troops are resting up in three different places, as a precaution, in case of artillery fire. And right he is! We hardly have time to eat when we hear a roaring sound in the air, followed by several frightful detonations. Huge clouds of smoke burst from our cannons. In a flash, our good gunners are there with their horses, racing at lightning speed down the hill with their cannons into a protective depression in the ground. Scarcely a few minutes have passed when a shell of very heavy caliber comes crashing down with huge force, right next to our 3rd Platoon. It seems to me that it hit dead center. It takes a while till the gun smoke has dispersed and the troops are visible again. Except for a few wounded, no damage is done.

At that moment a figure in earth-colored garb emerges from the underbrush. It is a Russian soldier with his rifle slung over his shoulder. Does he want to be taken prisoner? In that case he must throw away his rifle. By calling out to him and through gestures our company commander tries to make him understand that. He does not comply. Our commander alerts us to shoot if necessary. At that point, the Russian raises his rifle from about 80 meters away and starts shooting at our company. But fortunately he misses us. We are quite angry. This is becoming a serious matter. Command given to shoot the Russian! Not a single rifle goes off. We resent shooting at an individual under such unfair circumstances. But finally, aware that we are in danger ourselves, some of us fire a few shots. The Russian falls down but is still stirring; apparently he is wounded. A sergeant closes in and ends his life with a well-aimed bullet to his head. In silence we move down to the low ground past the bleeding corpse in the grass. A feeling of compassion for this poor man wells up in us, and we bow before the majesty of death. Fearlessly and loyally, this brave Russian soldier had fought to his last breath for Mother Russia until he had to submit to the harsh laws of war. Why didn't he throw away his weapon, and why did he still shoot when confronted by such superior force that he had to realize the hopelessness of his situation?

We now dug in next to a steep embankment to protect ourselves from artillery fire. Again a few Russians came out of the brush. With pale faces they ran toward us and surrendered. They were deathly afraid. Apparently they had seen what had happened to the Russian a few minutes ago. We took good care of them, gave them something to eat, then moved them on to the next field base. After a brief respite our march continued. The army marched northward on the main road in one long column until the evening shadows lengthened and fell on our tired bodies. Far from our loved ones, we were headed toward an unknown destiny. There was little hope that we would find a place to sleep tonight since we were still so close to the enemy. By now there was total darkness. The 10th Company was just getting close to a village before us (Ernstwalde?) when a huge machine gun fire let loose, hitting them and us, so that we hurried into the next ditch by the road.

Dust from the street was whipped up high into the air. One shot landed with a thud squarely on Lieutenant Meysenburg's backpack. The village before us was occupied by Russians. In the midst of infantry fire we continued to follow the 10th Company. With a loud hurrah they attacked the village from which the Russians were withdrawing in haste. You could hear wild screaming in the night. The shooting continued from both sides until we stopped at last before reaching the village, to get some rest on scattered heaps of straw. The exertions of the last few days had left us stiff and aching. But it took a while before we got to sleep. The field kitchen passed out some food, but we also had to get hold of some more straw. It was perhaps two o'clock in the morning when I walked to the farmhouse with a few of the men to get some water. The moon looked down upon the tall, ancient trees of the park and through misty clouds. The world lay there just as silent as the soldiers in gray on their stretchers by the wall, to be taken tomorrow by their comrades to their eternal resting place.

"Textbook Maneuvering"

I managed only two hours of sleep, as I kept shivering from the cold, my cape and the little bit of straw being of little use against the sharp autumn wind. I was glad when we got up and were able to warm ourselves with a cup of coffee from the field kitchen. And with the break of dawn we were once again on the move. We had to remain close on the heels of the enemy. At night strong Russian rear guards entrenched themselves once again in favorable positions near the "Kanzelberg" (September 11) to resume a strong defense. Bright and early we proceeded in open formation across fields, meadows, and through woods until our company finally came upon a rather high railroad embankment that traversed the terrain.

We quickly run across the tracks and scramble up another slope. Some bushes offer protection. Sssst! The first shells zigzag through the branches, small pits in the sand right in front of us! Cautiously we lift our heads. Above us hissing shells. Thunderous noise echoing from the hills. To the right of us our machine gunners move ahead, meter by meter, to flank the enemy. It's textbook maneuvering! With wild jumps we break out of our hiding places. The Russian machine guns are spitting out fire. A wild scream nearby. Someone is staggering. Another one drops his rifle and collapses. By now we have advanced 100 meters. We jump into a ditch. Let's catch our breath! Get up! Quick! Into the next trench. The Russians target our trench accurately. I take a quick look above the edge of the trench when—smack!—a bullet hits my helmet and bends its steel rim. The wounded are left behind.

At last our brigade is fighting in one line. We shoot with all our might until the barrels get hot. Our machine guns fire rapidly. We notice that we have gained the upper hand. We race down into the low terrain like crazy, all the while supported by our own strong artillery fire. Now we can clearly make out a Russian entrenchment. At that moment we can see white flags being hoisted in the enemy line as well as bayonets with white rags tied around them. Quite a few of the Russians jump back under cover as quickly as they can, but most of them come running towards us with their hands up high to give themselves up. It was a strange sight to see these figures in earth-tone clothes, with raised arms, come running toward us to surrender in seemingly never-ending numbers. Our troops were jubilant. Each one of them had experienced something out of the ordinary. One had a bullet stuck in his backpack, another had a helmet still intact even though it had been hit, and still another was saved from a direct hit by a notebook. In short, everyone had a different story to tell.

On September 12, 1914, we continued our forward march. The Russians had withdrawn in a hurry, but had nevertheless been under fierce attack by our 22nd Division near Gumbinnen [Map 4]. We were still far from Gumbinnen when some of the pilots told us, "Just wait till you come to Gumbinnen; it's not a pretty picture. They won't be back soon!" The closer we came to the city, the more frequently we encountered the debris left behind by an enemy who had retreated in a hurry and who had been followed on his heels by our troops. The streets were full of smashed ammunition carts, dead horses, bicycles, crushed automobiles. The city of

Gumbinnen showed the results of severe street fighting. A number of houses were still burning and only bare walls were visible under the open skies. In the streets were groups of Russian prisoners who had been ordered to extinguish the fire. And so we marched through the city singing, joyfully welcomed by the few people who had stayed there. Night had fallen by the time we left the last houses behind us. Before us lay a vast plain, stubble-fields, and cloud chasing cloud in the sky. A sudden storm became a veritable hurricane. In the distance we heard subdued sounds of rifle fire. On the dark horizon all around us we could see bright, vast conflagrations of fire, a truly overwhelming picture! Our march came to a halt; the artillery advanced. The enemy, according to scout reports, has dug new entrenchments. Tonight we were to drive them out of their positions with our bayonets. Soon we were told to stand at the ready. Unfortunately, the forthcoming attack would follow a long difficult march that had left us tired, dusty and hungry, but quite unexpectedly, the enemy moved on.

We set out at once to find overnight quarters. Finding shelter for my platoon wasn't easy, but there it was, a small deserted house. We had to force the doors open. The folks must have been poor. Everything was quite primitive. But at least we had a roof over our heads. So, late at night, we brewed ourselves a strong cup of coffee and when mail was distributed also, we were jubilant. A short period of rest followed, for early at the break of dawn we were called up to get going. The rain was coming down hard and we were knee-deep in mud. Day and night we continued marching, without pause.

On September 14 we came to a halt in an open field thinking we would bivouac. Suddenly there was activity from the other companies nearby and shouts of hurrah. Our company commander came and said, "The enemy is beaten and completely driven out of East Prussia." The command was given, "Unload, cover the muzzles! All band members to the front!" In high spirits we then proceeded to our quarters. One young musketeer asked hopefully, "Herr Leutnant, does this mean the war is over?" It was a good thing we didn't realize this was only the beginning.

The successful "Battle of the Masurian Lakes" resulted in 45,000 Russian prisoners of war and a large cache of weapons and war materials. Although this battle was not a second Tannenberg, the enemy had suffered heavy losses and would be unable to mount any sizeable operation for some time to come. East Prussia was liberated, its soil free from enemy forces.

Chapter Four

CAMPAIGN IN SOUTHERN POLAND (9TH ARMY),
SEPTEMBER, OCTOBER 1914

The Southeastern Theater of War, September 1914 [Map 6a]

The situation for the Austrian troops in the southeastern theater of war did not look rosy. Faced with the threat of being encircled after the second battle near Lemberg [Lvov] by the vastly superior Russian forces, the Austro-Hungarian army had retreated behind the San River in the Carpathian Mountains. Hungary and Silesia were in danger. For that reason Hindenburg was given orders by the military high command to transport by train to Silesia those forces that were no longer needed in East Prussia and to have them move against the flank and rear of the Russian armies.

On September 14 and 15, 1914, our troops got some well-deserved rest in the village of Patilszen [near Insterburg, East Prussia] [Map 4]. We were happy and in a good mood. The hosts we officers were staying with were friendly and helpful in any way possible. We used the time to get everything back in shape. As for me, I enjoyed being with Herr Hauptmann Pfannstiehl and the Lieutenants Lüttich and Bittorf. On Tuesday, September 15, I surveyed the area of the war-ravaged town of Stallupönen along with the chief physician, Dr. Rolle. It was a nice day, conducive to a leisurely walk along the road. In one house there were friendly artillery gunners inviting us to a glass of brandy so as to lift our spirits for the tour we were about to take. Before we knew it, we came upon signs that pointed to the field postal services, and we thought it would be interesting to take a look. Perhaps we hoped for some mail for ourselves. But there was nothing for us in the mailbag for Infantry Regiment 96. A large room was stacked high with mailbags, and each one of them had attached to it the number of the regiment. The work that this entails must have been tremendous, considering the tons of letters, cards, newspapers, parcels that are

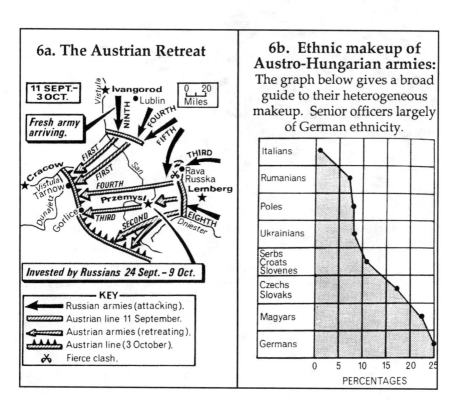

6a. The Austrian Retreat

11 SEPT.-
3 OCT.

Fresh army arriving.

0 20 Miles

Vistula

Ivangorod

Lublin

NINTH

FOURTH

FIFTH

FIRST

Cracow

FIRST

Vistula

Tarnow

FOURTH

San

THIRD

Rava Russka

Lemberg

Przemysl

Dunajetz

Gorlice

THIRD

SECOND

EIGHTH

Dniester

Invested by Russians 24 Sept. - 9 Oct.

KEY

Russian armies (attacking).

Austrian line 11 September.

Austrian armies (retreating).

Austrian line (3 October).

Fierce clash.

6b. Ethnic makeup of Austro-Hungarian armies:

The graph below gives a broad guide to their heterogeneous makeup. Senior officers largely of German ethnicity.

Italians

Rumanians

Poles

Ukrainians

Serbs
Croats
Slovenes

Czechs
Slovaks

Magyars

Germans

0   5   10   15   20   25

PERCENTAGES

Map 6a

The Austrian Retreat: September 11-October 3, 1914

After losing the "Battles of Lemberg," the Austro-Hungarian troops retreated west behind Przemysl and the San River to escape the advancing Russian troops.

Map 6b

Ethnic Make-up of Austro-Hungarian Armies

The Austrians could not always rely on their fellow soldiers, except for their German allies.

Street refuse is removed by a clean-up crew in a nice neighborhood of the village of Patilszen near Insterburg, East Prussia.

being sent into the field daily. The "postmen" appeared quite happy; you could tell they were well cared for here. We were now entering Stallupönen. The town had taken a severe beating. How we would have loved to enjoy a refreshing drink somewhere. We found instead rubble and ruins from incendiary bombs. There was hardly a house unscathed. We walked into a pharmacy. My companion hoped to find some things here with which to replenish the supplies in his ambulance. But this house, like all the rest, had been deserted by its occupants. The living quarters were in a sad state. Things were scattered everywhere and much was destroyed. In the town square we came across His Excellency, the Duke Heinrich XXVII of Reuss, as well as the heir apparent, Reuss, and the commanding general of the XI Artillery Corps, General Otto von Plüskow.

The next few days were spent marching at a moderate pace, but where these marches would take us we didn't know. We were pretty sure that we wouldn't stay much longer in East Prussia. On Friday, September 18, we reached Insterburg. It was in Insterburg where Rennenkampf had stayed to set up the administrative center of East Prussia. We marched on in pouring rain, until at last we reached Labian on the Baltic Sea.

Everywhere we saw shell craters, a familiar sight by now. On their forward march the Russians had come quite close to Labian. All around town the Germans had created strong defenses. We saw huge trenches with barbed wire barricades and others made with branches. Because of these the Germans had succeeded in keeping the enemy at bay. At last we were once again in a larger city that had remained completely unscathed. We were able to spend a few carefree hours here and even had some champagne. Friendly East Prussians, whose sons served on the Western Front, were our gracious hosts. We went out to do some shopping and get ready for the long train journey that lay ahead.

On Tuesday, September 22, 1914, around noon, the train—from Belgium—was waiting for us in the railroad station of Labian, ready for departure. For the third time we were headed toward an unknown destination. First we went northwest toward Königsberg. It was such a relief to pass through nice towns and villages not harmed by the war except for wire barricades and other fortifications. All looked peaceful, and friendly people waved to us. Via Elbring-Dirschau-Schneidemühl-Lissa-Breslau we went ever farther south until we reached Austrian soil near Oderberg. On September 24 the Carpathian Mountains were beckoning from a distance. Soon they were to become the scene of fierce fighting.

Krakau [Cracow] and Forward March

During our trip, on nearly all railroad stations, there was talk of heavy Austrian losses. By and large, the mood of our allies was rather depressed. During the night of September 24 we arrived in Krakau [Map M1]. The fortified city appeared to be in a deep sleep, and the sound of our marching feet echoed through this foreign town. A huge gate was unlocked and we marched to the large square of the Rudolf barracks. Since we were very tired, we slept soundly on straw in the rather dirty rooms of the barracks. My fellow officers and I got up the next morning not too late so that, before our departure, we could see something of the former residence of the Polish kings and the site where they were crowned and taken to their last resting place. We walked through an ancient city gate and on as far as the new theater. At the theater plaza we had a cup of coffee in a hotel where we saw Krakau's upper crust diligently perusing the newspapers in search of the latest events at the front. These reports were all the more important to them since the Russians might well lay siege to the city of Krakau. We then returned to the barracks in quite a hurry since our departure was imminent. Large numbers of German soldiers were milling about in the streets. It was a lively scene! In the barracks-square our men made friends with their Austrian fellow soldiers. It wouldn't be long before we would have to fight side by side.

We were soon off in high spirits, leaving Krakau on September 25, 1914. Once again we were in foreign territory. German street names disappeared, as well as German signs of firms and businesses. Residential houses became scarce, and we spotted the first thatched roofs of cottages belonging to the Polish working class. Well-screened cannon barrels were barely visible amidst the defenses that had put on their wiry garb some time ago. A well-tilled, undulating field lay before us. Anxious questions arose in many of our men as to what they would be faced with on Russian soil and what quarters they would find once they had crossed the Russian

In a Polish village, east of Krakau, in late September 1914. A primitive lever is used to draw water from a well.

border. We were to find out soon enough. For now we were marching forward along a main road; things weren't too bad, but when we moved onto unpaved country roads it was tough going, and once we came through villages we were practically mired in mud. We sank in to our ankles and the vehicles to their axles. We found quarters for our men in houses and barns as best we could. It wasn't too cold yet to sleep in barns and stables.

A Polish-Jewish Family at Home

With the company commander by my side, I knocked at the door of a Jewish family; the door was locked. We knocked again several times before a Polish Jew opened the door. He had a long beard, curls alongside his face, and wore a caftan and the characteristic covering on his head. As we walked in we were struck by the prayerful mood in this room. Many candles were burning and in one corner an old Jew was praying. It was the evening before the Sabbath. A young and pretty woman was breast-feeding her child. She looked at us, afraid and suspicious. However, since she spoke Yiddish, she helped us to communicate better. We bought bread and eggs from them and then we sat around comfortably with a cup of steaming hot tea in this Jewish home, glad to have found a roof over our heads after a strenuous march. Later we swept the room clean, put some straw on the floor, and soon were fast asleep. Usually we had to get up very early to be on our way, often around four o'clock in the morning.

We would have loved to sleep another hour. After this short rest we could feel our aching bones more than ever. Besides, our sleep had been a restless one. We were itching uncomfortably all over. Just a reminder that we were in Poland where bugs of one kind or another seemed to be everywhere. Often we'd jump up from our bed of straw to search for the "beast" on our body, then catnap for another hour before the game would start all over again.

Departure Rituals

We are tossing around restlessly. It must be early morning. Listlessly we are waiting for the orderly. What time will we have to leave? Someone is knocking at the door. "Is this the 4th Company?" someone shouts. It's the orderly and it is still pitch-dark. He pulls out a piece of paper and reads: "The division is ordered to advance. The regiment will take position at the intersection X at 5 a.m. The company will fall into formation at once." This is it! We jump out of bed or rather up from the straw-matted floor. The orderlies get everything ready for our departure. The wake-up call arouses the entire company. If there is time I'll grab a cup of tea and a piece of bread. The horses are already saddled. In half-darkness the company assembles in the street; the sergeant reports briefly; and we start marching on this damp morning, followed by combat equipment. The wagons grind their way through deep mud with the drivers skillfully maneuvering onto every bit of dry ground. We are marching along a creek lined with bushy willows. Our squadron is spread out because of the miserable road. A grey gloomy atmosphere surrounds us. Even the gray, shimmering, thatched roofs in the village reflect this mood. The sun is still fairly warm, but already the leaves are turning yellow, and in the morning a damp fog rises from the meadows.

On Saturday, September 26, 1914, we marched through valleys and across smaller hills until we reached our quarters toward evening before it was getting dark. This time we had a rather modern house; but because of the bugs we took all beds outside, swept the house clean, and then started cooking with abandon. The Poles were shy but not unfriendly. We managed to communicate by sign language. Soon we had memorized at least the most common words such as *Panje* [woman], *mleko* (*Milch*) [milk], etc. And whenever we came to an impasse we would ask a Jew to help us out. [Their Yiddish is close to German.]

The Nida River Basin in Southern Poland [Map M1]

Gradually we were approaching the enemy. When we marched by way of Miechow, Wodzislaw to Mobrowice on Sunday, September 27, we learned that Cossacks were nearby. The division followed along the main road in an eastern direction. On Monday our brigade (Brigade Manstein, Infantry Regiment 94 and 96) was to protect the right flank of the main body of our army and attack and drive back enemy troops. In cold, inclement weather we approached the bed of the Nida River. If the enemy was here at all, he had to be near the river. And that was the case, as we could tell from the brigade's frequent stops and the way the artillery was moving forward. We came closer and closer to mountainous terrain. The river meandered through the plains and was a lovely sight. Nestled on the side of the mountain was the Russian garrison of Pinczow. The area resembled somewhat the landscape around the city of Jena. The muffled roar of cannons firing told us the Russians were nearby. Protected by the river below, the Russians had set up their artillery in the mountains and were sending us their fiery volleys of "welcome." From the distance we

Good quarters at a Polish house. Author, *standing, third from left*, with ribbon in tunic. Note woman in doorway.

could see those pretty-looking tiny shrapnel clouds, high up at times, then again lower, clouds that looked so innocent yet could become so dangerous. Parts of our infantry advanced to cover the artillery, and now our cannons also started firing. We could not yet move ahead since we had no intelligence on the strength of the enemy. Besides, it seemed that our brigade general intended to wait until dark before making his next move.

Later in the afternoon our 4th Company received special orders; namely, to occupy a bridge on the Nida River and if necessary to clear it of enemy troops. Protected by low-growing shrubbery we

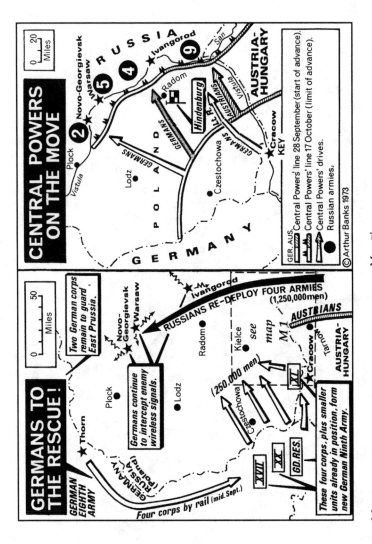

Map 7a

Germans to the Rescue!

Map 7b

Central Powers on the Move.

Hindenburg's new Ninth Army helped the Austrians push the Russian armies behind the Vistula River before massive Russian forces resumed a counterattack. (Map 7a includes "Inset" for Map M1.)

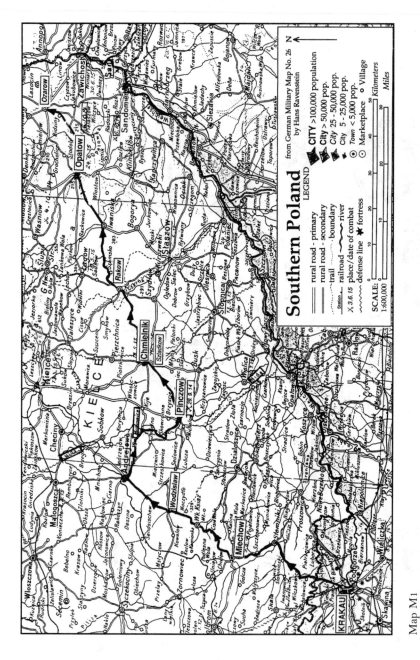

Map M1

German Military Map, 1914, of Southern Poland

Skirmishes and major engagements took place on their forward march between Krakau and Ozarow. Note dates of combat: 29-9-14 and 6–10–14. Any others belong to different campaigns. The Nida River Basin runs north–south, west of Kielce.

moved ahead across barren, sandy stretches of land where our wagons got stuck in the sand from time to time. It was no easy task to find our way through such a sandy desert where trails were easily covered up. Slowly we moved ahead accompanied by some of our dragoons [heavily armed mounted troops], always aware that we could run into the enemy any moment. In open position we finally came through a lovely wooded area down into the valley of the Nida River from where we had an unobstructed view of the entire region. The whole area seemed deserted, and where on earth was our regiment? Perhaps they were engaged in combat? Since the wind came from the opposite direction we could no longer hear any cannon fire. It started getting quite foggy and dreary. We stopped near the river; we had become tired and hungry. The field kitchen pulled up with its steaming food, and we settled in for a little rest on the marshy meadow. We had not been able to find the bridge. There just was none. And the dragoons had come up with nothing. Since there was no way to cross the rather wide river we had no choice but to stay on this side of its bank.

In the meantime, it had turned completely dark, and stormy weather was approaching. This was the time to seek cover in the next village, the troops as always in houses and barns while the dragoons were sent back to the regiment to let them know we would spend the night here and catch up with them the next morning. A farmer with whom we were staying overnight would show them the way. There we were, warm and cozy in our *Panje* [E. Panie] nest. We had come to use the word *Panje* for everything Polish. [*Panje* actually means "woman," not "Polish."] Thus we talked of *Panje* wagon, *Panje* horses, *Panje* coats, etc. The storm rattled the window panes, and dead tired we lay down on our beds of straw only to be awakened by the huffing and puffing of the returning *Panje* farmer who must have had a difficult time out there following our orders. He simply would not settle down until we finally managed to pick him up in his wet fur coat and fling him good-naturedly onto his bed. Presto—peace had been restored! Everybody fell asleep!

A lot had happened near Pinczow where troops were to cross the Nida River. That's where the battle had continued to create a bridgehead. Only one bridge led to the other side. The enemy had strategically placed gasoline-soaked straw under the arches of the wooden bridge. As the first group approached, the bridge went up in flames and machine gun fire rained down on it and on the path. Still, our men kept going. But the flames raced on and the danger grew. One company had already made it over, and so the entire brigade crossed over on the double. The crossing had been successful despite huge losses. Our good Colonel von Bonin was hit in both legs. The next morning our company, too, marched into the little town of Pinczow. At last I was lucky enough to find tolerable overnight quarters in the house of the sexton who had formerly been a servant to the Prince Montenovo in Vienna, hence spoke German fluently. The furniture was modern, but as in much of Poland, it was a bit messy here, too. Pinczow was a garrison town in the province of Kielce. Its inhabitants numbered at the time approximately 7,000—largely Jews, as in most smaller Polish towns. The streets in these towns were typically dirty and the houses in disrepair. On Wednesday, we left Pinczow toward mid-morning in the direction of Sladkow-Duzy. We had fulfilled our mission, which was to drive the enemy out of the Nida River area.

Near Chmielnik we were to rejoin the main body of the company. Enemy contingents were still about in the region, even showering us once with shrapnel, which was quite uncomfortable, to say the least. Once near Chmielnik, our company commander, von der Becke, was riding far ahead of the company. Suddenly an explosion! Shrapnel had burst right next to him. While to the left of us our company marched forward on the main road, we took cover behind sand dunes until the artillery fire subsided.

On October 1, 1914, our march continued through beautiful forested areas, always edging closer to the enemy. The cold season was approaching and we could feel it. Rainstorms were battering our faces. However, in the afternoon the sun was out again and warmed us with its rays filtering through the branches. Once again we were in a forest and stood at the ready late in the afternoon. Looking through my field glasses I surveyed the woods there before me, woods interspersed with green meadows and fields. Silhouetted against this background were the columns of troops marching forward and their staff officers sitting erect on horseback. The latest communication was of the enemy digging in near Potock. But these were retreating troops bivouacking at night, only to continue their flight in the morning. We therefore figured we were not in any danger and decided to look for quarters in Nowa Wies. The next morning we moved on to the town of Rakow. The land around it did not look very fertile since the soil consisted mostly of sand. Still, this was not a barren landscape. A small river meandered through the valley, turning the wheels of many a mill along its way. As the officer in charge, I posted guards along bridges and fords. We no longer observed any enemy movement. All was peaceful. This region seemed far removed from all civilization. There was no railroad connecting the village with the area's larger towns. These small hamlets like Rakow usually had rather wide streets and one very large regular market square which was filled today with all kinds of German vehicles, ammunition trains, artillery, etc.

Gradually we approached the Weichsel River [Wista/Vistula]. On Saturday, October 3, we ended up in Njazd. Above it on a hill were the ruins of a huge fairytale castle. The night sky was visible through row upon row of large windows, and the mighty towers by the gate were imposing.

Since new enemy corps were reported near Opatow we had to make sure the village was well protected. My platoon and I were sent to an outpost. Needless to say, we never got out of our uniforms all night. I spent the night in a house entryway that doubled as a chicken coop. A cold wind came through the doors. I was often roused by rifle fire, and early in the morning a rooster started crowing pitilessly. Was I glad when we were told to start marching!

It seems that on Sundays unusual events would take place. And so it was on October 4. We had quite an encounter with the Russians near Opatow. The cannons were already thundering early in the morning. Gradually our ranks went into open formation to get ready for combat. To begin with, each company was standing behind houses but then they all proceeded in extended lines across wide fields and old Russian trenches until we reached a hill from where we had an immense panoramic view.

German lines of skirmishers everywhere, puffy clouds of shrapnel dancing through the air, powder smoke and flashing artillery fire. The Russians surge forward to seek protection in the low-lying ground. Then flames are shooting upward up there on the hill. A Russian cannon is hit outright. Through our field glasses we see a second one under fire nearly breaking apart. The Russian infantry is gone, but now a cavalry contingent races up the hill to save the gun. Shells are hitting the ground nearby. We hold our breath while tensely watching the scene. They get up there double-quick and, lo and behold, these brave men succeed in saving the cannon. Some of the enemy troops escape, many are taken prisoner. As we cross the valley basin under infantry fire, our side has already taken hundreds of prisoners.

Toward evening we proceed slowly across the battlefield. Night is falling, mercifully covering all that misery and horror. The wounded lie by the hundreds between the dead. All choked up, we walk by, unable to give aid because we have to push forward without pause. A cold rain is beginning to fall. Shivering, we come to a halt in a field, searching in vain for a dry spot in which to settle down. The few blades of straw that we find to lie on are soon drenched so that there is no way of getting any real rest.

It wasn't until October 5 in Tominy that we found quarters again. Because of the heavy rains, the roads had turned into such a mess that our supply train had not been able to reach us. There was little bread left but we knew what to do. There was a baker in our company! We scrounged together enough flour and needed ingredients, even found an oven. Soon we were all busy baking bread, and it wasn't long before the entire house was filled with the aroma of freshly baked bread, which was then distributed to all men in the company. We stayed in Tominy until Thursday, October 7, 1914. At last we had enough time to wash our clothes and get everything back in shape. The *Panje* family, where we were staying, soon got tired of our hustle and bustle and departed voluntarily, which made it easier for us.

The weather was getting colder every day. Winter was on its way with cold rain and snow. The country roads turned into a soggy morass. On Friday, October 8, we came through Ozarow, a miserable place if ever there was one. The streets were in deplorable condition. It would have been easier to march somewhere in a ploughed field. Were we ever glad to leave this place behind! Next we passed through a stretch of sandy desert until groves of birch trees and small streams began to perk up the landscape, especially near Bronislawow and Lubowa. We stayed in Jadwigow near the Vistula River, where we finally were able to get some rest after having marched for days on end. We set up housekeeping in the few houses and nearby barns. that were available. Our *Panjes* vacated their homes for us, and we succumbed at last to a deep, long sleep.

During this constant rain the courtyard had gradually turned into a veritable lake. The manure pile in the middle contributed to the unpleasant conditions. We therefore proceeded to dig ditches, and a brown flood drained off so that we were now able to get in and out of the house without getting our feet wet. The gunners, who were bivouacking in the stable and the barn, were our good friends. We also improved the roads, sometimes to the distress of the village folks because we would help ourselves to bricks from masonry walls to use as macadam for the roads. Daily we anticipated mail, but in vain, because the wagons simply could not move on the roads. To think that we could have indulged in reading letters and newspapers now when we finally had a few days rest after our endless marches. Also we could have used food packages, for food was in scarce supply. Hardly a pig could be rounded up in this area, and cattle had to be rustled from far away.

Heavy fighting had broken out near the Vistula River while we had been spending peaceful days in Jadwigow. The Austrians tried to cross the San River [a tributary east of the Vistula River] while the Germans staged fake crossings along the Vistula River [Map 7b]. As a result we heard machine guns rattling and distant guns roaring, especially at night while searchlights fingered the darkness like ghosts. Once we, too, were called up suddenly. According to reports from our pilots, strong Russian columns were moving toward the Vistula. On Tuesday, October 13, at 9 p.m. we therefore left for Ozarow, where we arrived around midnight after navigating through sand and swamps. There we stayed as a reserve unit. The place was alive with troops, especially Austrians, who looked very picturesque in their colorful uniforms. Since the Russians did not come, however, we were able to return (shivering from the cold) to our quarters in Jadwigow.

An Uplifting Field Service

We had our first field service on October 11. The battalion formed one large square in the center of which stood the Chaplain von Stosch. Although the solemn arches beneath a church ceiling were missing and there were no uplifting sounds of an organ, the minister's words spoke directly to our hearts even though they were accompanied by the roar of the cannons way down, near the Vistula River. At this point most of our group were still alive; Death, the Reaper, had not yet taken in his rich harvest from us. What would the future hold? When will we be engaged in combat once again? Will I, too, have to confront my maker soon? And we found solace in the words of this consoling song:

> DER HERR IST NUN UND NIMMERMEHR VON SEINEM VOLK GESCHIEDEN; ER BLEIBET IHRE ZUVERSICHT, IHR SEGEN, HEIL UND FRIEDEN. MIT MUTTERHÄNDEN LEITET ER DIE SEINEN STETIG HIN UND HER. GEBT UNSERM GOTT DIE EHRE!

> THE LORD WON'T NOW OR NEVERMORE BE SEPARATED FROM HIS FLOCK; HE REMAINS THEIR HOPE AND PEACE, THEIR BLESSING AND SALVATION! HE GUIDETH THEM WITH TENDER CARE WHEREVER LIFE MAY TAKE THEM. GLORY BE TO OUR GOD!

Chapter Five

RETREAT AND ATTACK: THE BATTLE OF LODZ
NOVEMBER 1914

While my father's 96th Infantry Regiment was fighting the Russians in Southern Poland near the Vistula River [Weichsel R., Map M1] and largely contained the enemy, the Austro-German advance collapsed near Warsaw and Ivangorod, forcing their armies to retreat. My father's regiment had been ordered to march north from Ozarow [Map 8a] to Radom when they were caught up in the general retreat.

Face to Face with Field Marshal Paul von Hindenburg

At last, on Saturday, October 17, 1914, we received orders for our departure. A change on a grand scale in the disposition of troops must have been under way, judging from the continuous stream of Austrian troops marching by, day after day. The rains had subsided, and in beautiful autumn weather we were able to march vigorously every day. On October 19 we managed more than 50 kilometers. Were we surprised when we noticed that we were moving more and more in a western direction, which meant we were retreating! The following day we marched through Radom, the regional seat of government. At last we were to see Hindenburg face to face. We marched past him in spirited goose-step. There he was before us! His robust, powerful body and his energetic facial features exuded the kind of willpower and strength needed to conquer the enormous difficulties he was encountering at this time.

The Eastern Front in October 1914

The general situation in the theater of war was as follows: By marching continually we had reached the Vistula, somewhere north of the mouth of the San River. The Russians had retreated behind the Vistula but were

Map 8a

The Russian Advance, October 17–November 10, 1914

As part of the Ninth Army, Lt. R. and his regiment were forced to withdraw from Radom inside Poland as far as the German border. The Ninth Army then "switched" position to the north for a massive counteroffensive, beginning on November 10, 1914 (November 11, according to Lt. R.).

constantly being re-enforced. In heavy fighting, the XI Corps, the guard reserve corps, and the XX Prussian Corps along with Austrian troops prevented the Russians from pushing forward near Ivangorod [northeast of Radom]. Hindenburg in the meantime, in mid-October, fought valiantly southwest of Warschau [Warsaw] with the bulk of the 9th German Army, where they were pitted against the 4th, 5th, and 2nd Russian Armies advancing from Warsaw and Nowo Georgiewsk. But the enemy was too powerful. The combined German-Austro-Hungarian forces were unable to hold the line near Ivangorod, and in the north the massive Russian forces southwest of Warsaw numbering more than 10 A.K. [Army Corps] were threatening to outflank the left wing of the 9th German Army. Therefore, Hindenburg had to make the difficult decision to retreat.

And now the immense Russian steam roller was set in motion. The allies touted this huge withdrawal as a big victory. Crushing any and all resistance, the Russian steamroller would grind its way across Germany and the Austro-Hungarian lands. The enemy was already in high hopes that by Christmas they would be able to dictate their peace. And, indeed, these overly optimistic hopes of our adversary were not totally unjustified. Opposite three million Russians we had only one million soldiers on the entire front between the Carpathian Mountains and the Baltic Sea. The mighty middle section alone, under the Russian General Ruski, was pouring westward with 25 corps. It was reported to Hindenburg's headquarters that Nikolai Nikolajewitsch, the Russian supreme commander, had ordered his main contingent of troops to head toward Silesia to take possession of that region so rich in coal and iron and so important to us in Germany.

Hindenburg realized that he would not be able to stop the advancing tide of Russian troops by taking a stand along the entire German border. They would soon overcome all resistance. No, the salvation would lie not in defending the borders, but in staging an all-out attack against the weaker north wing of the enemy with the aim of destroying it, which might result in unraveling the entire Russian battlefront. That was Hindenburg's new stratagem.

The following days we were marching again. The cool fall air was more and more noticeable. The trees were shedding their leaves. It wouldn't be long now before winter set in. This thought was a matter of concern to all of us. So far we couldn't complain, for the crisp autumn air was conducive to vigorous marching. But the nights were bitter cold, as we spent them in barns or stables or even out in the open air. We gradually approached the rather densely populated area around Lodz [Lvov]. Many Germans lived there so that village after village almost looked like home. Moreover, most names on houses and inscriptions at the cemetery were in German. One Sunday, to our great surprise, we heard this song from a Protestant village church, "Allein Gott in der Höh' sei Ehr" ["Glory Be to God Alone on High"]. Accompanied by the organ, these words rang out on this clear autumn day:

EIN WOHLGEFALLEN GOTT AN UNS HAT, NUN IST GROSS FRIED OHN UNTERLASS, ALL FEHD HAT NUN EIN ENDE.

GOD'S GOOD WILL IS BESTOWED UPON US, FOR NOW THERE WILL BE PEACE FOREVER, ALL FEUDS ARE COMING TO AN END.

Ah, these poor German folks! For them the war wouldn't be over for a long time. Two months hence they would really feel the hardships of war. Many of these villages would be razed to the ground.

On October 25 we quartered in Wisniewa Gora. This is a kind of summer resort for the people of Lodz. The houses here have more of an urban look. We made ourselves at home in a beautiful villa that was abandoned by its owners. It had been a long time since we had been able to do any real cooking, and so we prepared our favorite dish, potato salad. With a cup of coffee we lounged around on elegant sofas, but such luxury didn't last long. An alert reached us after only a few short hours of rest. The enemy had followed on our heels.

The Russian Attack Near Strykow

On October 26 we were in the village of Lupiny ready to fight again, but for the night we were lucky enough to quarter in Moskev, before pushing forward to Strykow on October 27 [Map 8a]. As rear guard, we were to safeguard the departure of our regiment. In closed formations we advanced through hilly terrain, past a factory on marshy grounds. On a hilltop we changed into skirmishing order. With my platoon I took position along the street leading to Strykow, whose church tower served as a guide post. I had reached a wooded area when not far behind us our cannons started roaring; our immediate reflex was to acknowledge it with a respectful bow! Finally we reached Strykow. A strangely oppressive calm had settled over the town. We saw very few people in the streets. One Jew told me that the Russians had left the village only a short while ago. I therefore sent out several teams to search houses and barns thoroughly while I stayed behind for a while, waiting near a rather beautiful church building still under construction. It was by now late afternoon, and the company was given orders to occupy the left side of the road near the village exit. We moved into position and got our rifles ready to fire, but detected no enemy movement. We had gone without food the entire day because the field kitchen had been left behind, and a search in our haversacks turned up nothing. We went off into the village to search for bread and were lucky to find enough for all to share. It was already getting dark, and we toyed with the idea to find night quarters in a nearby barn, when a shot pierced the air not far from us. Another followed. We dismissed these as just another "shooting game" by our patrols. But the firing increased and seemed to be spreading. Darkness had set in by now. We grabbed our rifles, and two platoons took up positions to the left and right of the barn on the outskirts of the village. I was standing behind the barn with the rest of the company. The fire increased more and more; bullets were hitting the ground before us. And now our machine guns let loose, as the entire place and everything around it came alive. The enemy seemed to be everywhere, shooting from every corner and from every house. Suddenly a bright blaze of fire: Burning houses lit up the scene of combat with blood-red flames. There were loud hurrahs even close by. Our front line drew back on reflex. We weren't sure who was out there. The hurrahs were misleading. Was it possible that our own troops might have attacked us in the darkness? The sound of many voices came from both sides. Foreign-sounding words fell upon our ears. Now there was no doubt: the Russians were right in front of us! Suddenly they were jumping from behind the barn only a few steps away from us. Fiery shots burst forth from our gun barrels. Bloodsoaked, the wounded right in front of us were groaning and moaning. We, too, had incurred losses, but the attack was repelled. Step by step the Russians withdrew, but we also vacated the village.

Protected by a small rear guard we marched up the road. From there we sent the Russians a few more fiery greetings in the shape of several artillery salvoes. With a hissing sound the shells exploded in the village. Bursts of fire rose to the sky immersing the entire area in its red blaze. It was pitch dark when we continued our march along miserable roads. Every bone in our bodies ached from the exertion and nervous exhaustion. It was a miracle that the vehicles were moving forward at all in the deep sand. It wasn't until early morning that we finally stopped for temporary quarters in Kulonka. These were so crammed that we had trouble getting everyone sheltered. We had to hunker down in barns and stables almost like cattle. And again the following night there was no rest for the weary. Near Moderzew we had to dig trenches in which we finally fell asleep in the open air on a handful of straw, dead tired. During all that time we knew very well that the advancing enemy could attack at any time. At dawn we were up and off again, moving westward. We didn't know why we were withdrawing.

The German Aspect of the City of Lodz

On October 29 the chimneys of the city of Lodz appeared on the horizon. We were approaching the outskirts of the city. A nice forest gradually turned into a large park. We were welcomed by small blue-ribboned ponds with graceful bridges. German inscriptions reminded us that we were reaching a city that was almost half German. Endless German trenches were in place on the outskirts of the city, and our cannons were forever rumbling to deter the enemy. The suburbs of Lodz were extremely dirty and neglected. The brown wooden houses and the miserable streets were no different from those of small rural towns in Poland. The streets weren't paved; there were hardly any sidewalks; and the street lights were very poor. Most of the townspeople were laborers. As everywhere in Poland, Jews made up a large part of the population. They were good at peddling their wares when we were marching through.

There was something unfinished about this city. This comes as no surprise considering the fact that in the early 19th century it was still a village of approximately 800 inhabitants until it took a leap forward and blossomed through the business sense of German manufacturers so that within 100 years the population grew to about half a million, 40% of which was German. We found the Petrikaner St., all of 10 kilometers long, quite magnificent. With its traffic and beautiful boutiques it resembled somewhat the Friedrichstrasse in Berlin. Almost everyone spoke German and the children of the poor weavers were begging, "Lieber Herr, geben Sie uns doch bitte einen Groschen. Der liebe Gott vergelte es Ihnen." ["Dear sir, won't you please give us a penny, may the dear Lord repay you."] Many a soldier opened his heart, and the "German Barbarians" tossed many a coin to these poor children. Since all factories were out of commission, the population suffered greatly, even though relief organizations were trying hard to improve their situation.

Around noon we reached Widzewo [Map 8a], a blue-collar suburb of Lodz. It was extremely difficult to find quarters for everyone since the workers—all Germans—had nothing more than one room, a den, and a kitchen. I was fortunate in that I ended up in the home of an elderly lady who, it appeared, belonged to the middle class. Her husband, a factory director, had escaped to Moscow, leaving her alone with two daughters and an old mother. Finally a touch of civilization. We relaxed together in their sitting room and relished our noon meal served by the ladies themselves. What a blessing it was to be able to nap for an hour or so on a comfortable sofa. In the afternoon we had a cup of Russian tea and passed the time in stimulating conversation with the ladies. How wonderful, how refreshing this hour appeared to us after the enormous exertions and deprivations of the last few weeks. We were hopeful that we might be able to stay here until the next day and lounge around comfortably in soft, upholstered chairs.

Retreat [Map 8a]

Then suddenly a muffled thud! The cannons out there were starting to speak. More shots followed. Our ladies ran—pale as death. We had to get going at once, and within half an hour the battalion was ready to march. The pandemonium that ensued among the Lodzers was indescribable: in the streets everything went topsy-turvy; everyone seemed to be yelling—women, children, and men. With beds and other necessary household items, they ran wildly into the city or out into the open fields. At first there was no immediate danger. Advancing Russian troops came within range of our machine guns. The Russians did not respond, probably because they did not want to engage in potentially destructive artillery combat so close to the city. At dusk we left the metropolis of Poland, singing along the way, and late at night we found quarters in Ruda. The next morning we entrenched south of Lodz. All roads were filled with departing German troops. We, too, wouldn't stay long since the Russians were right on our heels. We soon marched toward Pabianice. The Russians followed slowly. It seems they could not hurry since our combat engineers had totally destroyed all bridges, railroad stations, and other means of transportation behind us. We soon came to the busy industrial town of Pabianice. Here, too, the German influence was strong, judging from the many German signs and the imposing Protestant church. People were buying and selling in the market place, and the peddlers didn't do badly with the soldiers passing through.

By now it was November, and the weather had become colder and quite stormy. The days were growing short and winter was fast approaching. No wonder we were in a depressed mood. And what was the reason for our enormous retreat? Had our army suffered a big defeat somewhere? We had to ask ourselves these questions again and again. On November 1, we were the advance guard on a small river near My-Luky. Enemy cavalry troops roamed the area. We were to prevent their crossing the river. We therefore set about destroying bridges. We barricaded shallow parts of the river to prevent their fording across, protecting these same areas

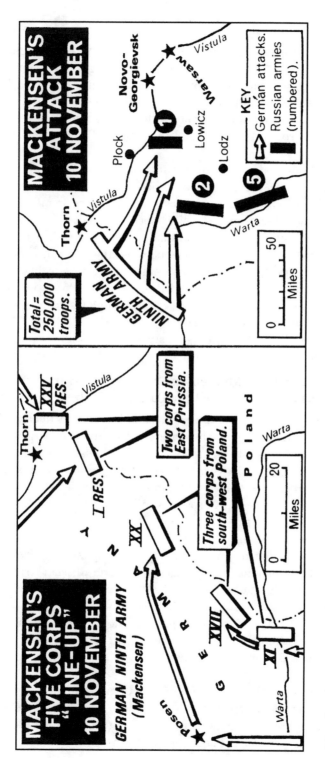

Mackensen's Five Corps "Line-up" and Attack

Map 8b

with guards and trenches. It was another restless and stressful night; not only were we tired out from all the marching, trying to make the river area safe put an additional burden on us, exhausting us even more. I was so glad when I was able to stop at a *Panje* house for a while and get a glass of milk. The house was quite a scene, with soldiers and local men and women all in one room! It was a good thing we had to move on before dawn.

We got closer and closer to the German border, crossing it near Grabow with a loud "hurrah" on November 5, 1914. Soldiers from the "Landsturm" defense force [a special reserve unit] were standing guard and they had dug a few trenches. All at once the landscape was transformed: no more bottomless sand and mud, but instead well-maintained roads. Here at the border the difference between the two sides was dramatic. The pretty rural town of Grabow was there before us like a little jewel compared to the Polish places of similar size. We approached Jarotschin on beautiful, well-kept roads, came through Ostrowo and were back on Polish-Russian soil near Peisem on the Warthe River [Warta River] by November 11. Our retreat westward had come to an end. We were once again assuming the offensive.

General von Mackensen's Strategy of War
(November 1914) [Map 8b] and the Battle of Lodz [Maps 9a, 9b]

The divisions of the cavalry on both sides had already duelled hard. The 11th of November was the date set by General August von Mackensen, leader of the 9th Army, for the general push forward against the right flank of the 2nd Russian Army. In the operation against Lodz the commander in chief intended to begin with a surprise attack and the annihilation of the V Siberian Corps near Wlozlaw. Our I and XXV Reserve Corps were to face the enemy's front, the XX with a movement to outflank the enemy, the army's cavalry corps against sides and back.

This extensive German attack came as a complete surprise to the Russian General Scheidemann, the leader of the 2nd Russian Army. In a brilliant attack, the German cavalry pushed General Novikow from Staw back to the Warta, and the Russian cavalry and infantry were driven out of Turek [Map 9a]. The German corps in the north had been locked in battle with the Russians as early as November 11, and the western section of Wlozlaw was already in German hands on November 12, together with 12,000 prisoners. Lipno was taken.

On November 14 the Russian Supreme Command had ordered the army to attack on the northwest front, to push deep into Germany and take over the line Ivrothschin-Ostrowo-Kreuzberg-Kattowitz [along the western Polish-German border]. The troops under Mackensen were already

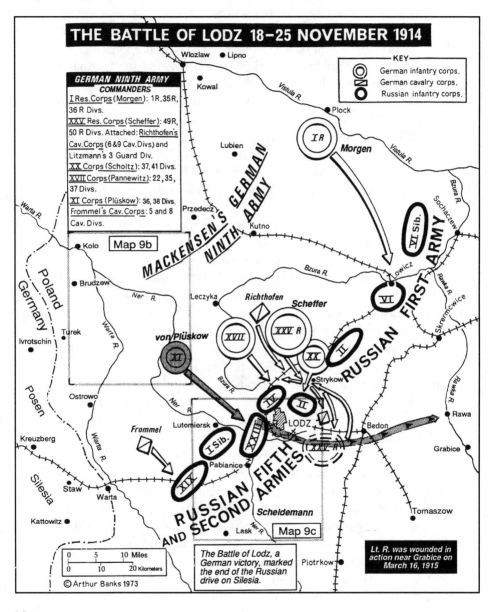

THE BATTLE OF LODZ 18–25 NOVEMBER 1914

KEY
- German infantry corps.
- German cavalry corps.
- Russian infantry corps.

GERMAN NINTH ARMY
COMMANDERS
I Res. Corps (Morgen): 1R, 35R, 36 R Divs.
XXV Res. Corps (Scheffer): 49R, 50 R Divs. Attached: Richthofen's Cav. Corps (6 & 9 Cav. Divs.) and Litzmann's 3 Guard Div.
XX Corps (Scholtz): 37, 41 Divs.
XVII Corps (Pannewitz): 22, 35, 37 Divs.
XI Corps (Plüskow): 36, 38 Divs.
Frommel's Cav. Corps: 5 and 8 Cav. Divs.

Map 9b

The Battle of Lodz, a German victory, marked the end of the Russian drive on Silesia.

Map 9c

Lt. R. was wounded in action near Grabice on March 16, 1915

© Arthur Banks 1973

Map 9a

The Battle of Lodz

Lt. R. belonged to the XI Corps, 38 Division, under General von Plüskow.

manning the line Brudzew-Kolo-Przedecz-Lubien-Kowal by the evening
of November 13 [some 60–90 miles east of border]. A look at the map
reveals how devastating a push by the 9th German Army into the rear of
the Russian army would be if Nikolai Nikolajewitsch was going to stick
to his plan of an offensive toward Silesia-Posen. And the German decision not to leave its 9th Army positioned near Czestochowa and thereby
extending the German front line, was absolutely correct. The Russians
were forced into a line of defense and had taken up strong holding positions. Our fliers were busy locating the Russians in their line Chelnino-
Grabina-Drewce in front of our XI Army Corps [Map 9b]. General von
Plüskow ordered our 38th Division to move head-on against the front,
the 22nd against the right wing near Drewce and then to loop around
near Glembokie.

On November 13, we stayed one more night in Ruszkow where we
got our marching orders at six o'clock the next morning. Something big
seemed to be in the air. On the way we encountered numerous medical
teams. We saw the Commanding General von Plüskow on horseback along
with the princely entourage and the rest of the staff. It was warm and
nice outside once again, and we stopped for a while in nearby woods, just
as in a maneuver. Forgetting all, we ate, drank, and talked to each other,
while relaxing on soft, mossy mounds under the trees. After a long separation, I found myself reunited with dear old friends, even from other
regiments who treated me to all kinds of savory tidbits. What if we had
known that this would be the last time for us to be together? (Lieutenants
Fromm and Voigt III./96) One of them would give his life for the father-
land the same evening.

All at once we had to start marching. The artillery was rumbling
already. "The success of this day depends on the successful attack by the
XI Corps," we were told. They were dragging huge cannons through the
woods. The Russians had dug deep, fortified entrenchments near Chelnino
[Map 9b]. We were advancing in platoon formation, then in single file
across a creek, up the slope from where open formations of the III Battalion were advancing. Already shrapnel fire was whistling above our heads.
On the outskirts of the village we stopped and crouched down in the
grass to avoid the fast-flying bullets. Right in front of us a soldier was hit
and collapsed. The medics took him to a nearby barn. In order to set up
an observation post, I went over to a farmhouse, together with our Company Commander von der Becke, the sergeant, and the rest of the troop
leaders. The infantry fire increased, patches of straw from the roof of
the house were sailing through the air. Jets of water were kicked up from

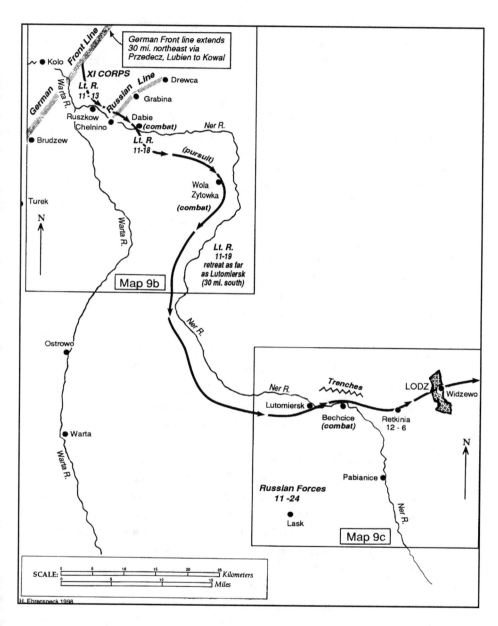

Maps 9b, 9c

Advance and Retreat

These maps show the combat routes taken by Lt. R.'s division, as part of the XI Corps, in the battle for the city of Lodz.

the pond, scaring ducks and geese and getting them aflutter. A pig running around aimlessly was hit in the leg and began to limp and scream
pitifully. Black clouds from hard hitting shells rose up high, resembling
huge trees, and smaller shrapnel clouds were literally dancing all over.
Teams of medics came and went to get the wounded out of the front
lines. We raced across the street with bullets whizzing by, barely missing
us and whipping up little dust clouds the moment they hit the ground.
We tried to assess the situation, but failed since we couldn't see very well.
The one thing we did see was our heavy shells crashing down near the
river. We were placed in the second attack line.

Around four o'clock we were given the signal to fix our bayonets.
Every single line was getting ready to advance and attack. In Chelnino, in
the meantime, our soldiers had been engaged in heavy fighting until the
Russians were forced to withdraw toward evening. Our comrade Lieutenant Fromm was killed in this battle. The village was ours. We stacked our
rifles against farm houses that were still smoldering and lay down in some
straw in the Russian trenches to catch our breath. It was a ghastly sight
to see the evening sky lit up by the burning buildings. The entire estate
was going up in flames. This was no time to relax. In order to be able to
attack the Russians that same evening this side of the Ner River and to
keep them unsettled, we started marching with fixed bayonets, after a
short rest, along the Chelnino-Dabie country road. We had hardly left
Chelnino when we were showered with shells, rocks and earth by a barrage of machine gun fire.

Night had fallen and so, of course, we couldn't see the enemy. We
groped along inside a ditch by the road until the fire ceased. A dead officer was lying in the field. I walked up to him and recognized to my
horror that it was our battalion commander, Colonel Böttiger. The night
had turned cold and windy and I had neither a coat nor a wrap with me; I
did not own an undervest either. Shivering all over from the cold, I wrapped
my orderly's tarp around me. From a fallen soldier we appropriated a rifle
with fixed bayonet and took off into a foggy night. In the fields and in
bushes we heard wounded Russians groaning and mumbling their "Jesus,
Maria..." throughout the night until we finally reached Dabie in the morning. Here we made a thorough search for Russian troops that might be
hiding somewhere, before seeking shelter in houses ourselves. We were
utterly exhausted and dropped off to sleep in a stupor. For days now we
had been engaged in battle and endured a great deal of stress. These
battles had resulted in heavy losses, but had not been in vain, for the

Russian corps, defeated, had to give up its positions north of the Ner River and was now on the other side of the river.

We expected counterattacks any time. We had been sound asleep for about two hours when we were suddenly roused by heavy gunfire. We had to get out and occupy the hills near the Ner River. Everywhere we looked there were German artillery and infantry on the move. From up here we had the Ner valley under control. The Russians tried to hold on to the bridgehead near Dabie and to force their way across the river Ner. From our vantage point above, the following spectacular scene unfolded before our eyes: On both sides the artillery was firing harder than I had ever experienced. Countless shrapnel clouds rolled over Dabie. Incendiary bombs came crashing down on roofs. Again and again infantry fire was cracking wildly, until it gradually weakened and died with the onset of dusk. It was once again quiet. The Russians had been unsuccessful in their attempts to break through and were therefore forced to withdraw under cover of night. We followed on November 18, crossed the river, and by doing so passed one section of the battlefield. Row upon row of dead Russians were lying there trapped by sudden death, a rigid hand still gripping a cartridge and ready to load, as if they were still alive. Others lay there limp, like tattered pieces of cloth.

On November 18 the army issued a favorable report regarding our situation. We were justifiably hopeful that we would succeed in encircling the enemy. The Corps Posen and Corps Breslau were to move up from the southwest and west. HKK 3 [German cavalry corps] were to take on Wadlewo in the south. Our XI Corps and the XVII (West Prussian) were to contain the enemy from the front by attacking, and the XX and the XIV Reserve Corps were to attack and deploy in the east while the Cavalry Corps Richthofen would close the encirclement in the region around Pidtskow [Map 9a]. If this operation turned out to be successful it was expected that a battle would take place on November 20, 1914, near Lodz, the Manchester of the east, similar to the battle of Tannenberg that Hindenburg had won on August 28, 1914.

It was an overcast day when we crossed the Ner River on November 18, 1914 [Map 9b]. The marshes were thick with fog. Trying to get across a sand-covered area became extremely difficult, a maneuver we hadn't tackled for a long time. For that reason we inched forward, very slowly, and came to a longer halt every quarter of an hour. The enemy seemed to be very close. Our advance guard was perhaps fighting them already. Some cavalry troops passed by with a few Russian prisoners. We came through bigger forests where different units stood at the ready. The

wireless operations went into action with their telegraph mast. This mast
was on wheels and could be rolled up or down within seconds. Russian
formations were seen nearby. But soon they seemed to have left and we
moved on. Shots were fired and shrapnel exploded here and there. We
were moving forward, in skirmishing order, and did not close ranks until
total darkness had fallen. We were ordered to push through as far as
Pabianice at any cost [southwest of Lodz]. We knew we couldn't count
on getting a night's rest.

Again and again, our forward march was interrupted by lengthy
stops due to congested roads caused by all the troops. Besides, the dark
night made it extremely difficult to see where we were going; at times we
had to leave the main road and find our way through swamps and fields.
At last it became easier and we were able to speed up a bit. It was an eerie
night. We could hardly make out the road now. In the woods we heard the
cracking of gunfire. We had to be almost in touching distance of the
enemy. In the distance a farm building was on fire and dimly lit the night.
To the left, far away, artillery fire was roaring, and the ceaseless high-
pitched sounds of infantry fire reached our ears. The night was pitch
dark. We had to watch our steps carefully so as not to stumble. "Walk
ahead of me in your light-colored coat, otherwise I can't see anything,"
von der Becke, our company commander, called out to me. I did walk
ahead, but he skidded down a high embankment anyway. A light blanket
of snow covered the fields, giving us a glimmer of light. Around midnight we came through a village. Shots rang out! What on earth was
happening? Perhaps Russian outposts? Still, we didn't let this stop our
forward march. Late at night we arrived in the village of Wola Zytowka
[Map 9b]. It was the 19th of November. A deadly silence covered the
village. We walked all the way through to the other end where our company was assigned quarters.

Then, all of a sudden, a terrible bang, a tremendous infantry fire!
With a rattling sound the bullets crash against the walls of houses and
barns. We throw ourselves to the ground or jump behind a cover. We
cannot see the enemy. Our men set a barn ablaze. Screaming, the occupants run with their cattle in tow. They are German settlers. Gradually
the infantry fire diminishes. We are inclined to believe that we have before us only smaller Russian contingents, perhaps only a detached group
of Cossacks...

We therefore decided to get some rest despite the fact that the enemy
was nearby. The people assured us that there weren't any Russians hiding
in the village. We searched everywhere and found nothing suspicious. We

stopped at a house where we found some milk, and we drank and drank until we could hold no more. We were hungry and fatigued. I told my platoon to stack their rifles in the farm yard and come into the house, while I went to get further orders from the company commander. By that time it was probably two o'clock in the morning. All of a sudden, the Russians started shooting again. Machine guns began rattling in other parts of the village. "Enough," we thought. "We've got to find out where exactly the enemy is holing up." We climbed up an embankment near the edge of the village. The enemy fire increased more and more. For us to attack during the night seemed hopeless, since we knew nothing about the strength of the enemy. It seemed they were shooting from fortified positions. We therefore returned to the village.

The company commander issued the following orders, "Two of the platoons will remain in the houses as reserves ready to fight, the third platoon will take position in open formation on the outskirts of the village." That order was for me, the leader of the third platoon; not much to look forward to. There we were on this cold November night, crouching outdoors in damp grass. Grey swaths of fog were rolling in and I pulled my cape around me tight, shivering in the cold and dead-tired. Now everything was quiet again. One could hear only the soft, crackling sound of burning houses, and their dying flames spread a dim light on the scene. We dug a make-shift trench barely deep enough to support our rifles and arms. Slowly morning was dawning. A deep silence surrounded us. At times we dropped off to a half-sleep, with a few men standing guard. Then, suddenly, we were wide awake. A nerve-shattering blast pierced the air. In a flash the Russians let loose a barrage of gunfire. Shells were raining down on us. The small, shallow trenches we had dug during the night saved us. Barely missing us, the downpour of shells zoomed above our heads into the barns and houses where the rest of the company was holed up. We remained glued to the ground. It was impossible to receive any further orders.

After about half an hour I saw German troops advancing, as well as machine guns and artillery. Since more lines of soldiers were advancing to the right of us, I decided the time had come for us to get out and move forward without awaiting special orders. "Move out on the double!" In an instant we were ducking behind the next rise in the ground which offered us some protection. But our situation was anything but comfortable. Bullets were passing over our heads so closely that they often hit the metal mess kits in our backpacks. Now we, too, suffered losses. There was nothing we could do to help the wounded around us. Spade in hand, the troops were digging in furiously. Since I didn't have a spade, I had to wait until one became available. Until then I was literally glued to the rise in the ground near the road. At last we succeeded, despite enemy fire, to finish digging a shallow trench.

By now it was perhaps noontime and the field kitchen could not possibly show. Our haversacks were completely empty. During our advance we had indeed sustained losses. The hillside behind us was covered with the dead and wounded. One soldier came running with ammunition when he was hit and fell down. With a pain-stricken face he grabbed his wounded chest and called out, "Water, water." We returned the enemy fire with volley after volley, and our artillery fired one shell after another into an enemy trench and caused huge black clouds of smoke to rise. We noticed a letup in enemy activity and were about ready to attack and throw the Russians out of their positions. But this was not to be.

Surprise Retreat

The Russians had attacked the wings of our brigade with such superior force that our battalions could no longer resist. Despite heavy fighting and heroic perseverance, especially by our artillery gunners, our forces had to give up their positions around four o'clock in the afternoon and retreat under heavy enemy pressure. An orderly came running, shouting breathlessly, "By order of the brigade commander: All troops will withdraw!" At first I thought I wasn't hearing right. But then I saw the sections next to us running back, and when I noticed an increase in enemy fire we, too, jumped out of our trench and raced down the hillside. A veritable hail of bullets was now whizzing about us. Many soldiers dropped to the ground. I was running as fast as I could over dead bodies and wounded until I reached the village. Here I threw myself down behind a house, completely out of breath. Thanks to my quick feet and by the grace of God I had come out of this alive. As I was continuing on across the fields I saw the fleeing masses of our regiment everywhere as far as I could see. If the Russians were to push on now it might mean the end of us. What luck that it was getting dark.

A stout fellow from Mecklenburg with robust red cheeks joined me, very chipper, without showing any sign of alarm at our critical situation. "Look there," he said smiling, "the 94th is retreating." Another fellow was running barefoot across the fields; he had taken off his shoes and socks, and in the rush of the retreat had had no time to put them on again. So there he was running barefoot, running and running. Despite these curious happenings, our situation was anything but funny. We had to expect the Russian advance troops any moment. I finally ran into the orderly who was leading his company commander's horse. And soon I found the company commander himself. We shook hands, happy to see one another. At dusk we withdrew a bit further, all the while collecting more men from our company—as much as this was possible. Order was restored fairly fast and at first the Russians didn't pursue us. For about an hour we marched and then, as we were so fatigued and hungry, stopped in order to dig a defense position for the night. An ice cold wind was whistling across the hills. Dead tired, some of us threw ourselves down on the hard ground, others stood around with their hands deep in their pockets, stamping the ground with their feet to escape the cold. And then suddenly red-hot flashes were zigzagging through the air, distant at first, then coming closer and closer. The Russians were covering the area with shrapnel. An explosion followed, screaming and moaning! One explosive had landed dead-center in our company, killing one man and wounding several others.

But we had to hurry to finish our entrenchments! It was pitch-dark by now. The Russians had stopped firing, which allowed us to rest up from all the exertion. Crouched as we were in a corner of our foxhole, without straw and without any covers, we were exposed to the ice-cold November air and yet managed to sleep a little. A corporal and two men were standing guard some 500 meters from us on one of the farmsteads. In case of a Russian attack one barn was to be set on fire. Oh, what losses we had suffered during these last few hours! At least a quarter of our contingent had been lost. Many were dead, others who were wounded—among them my orderly—were left behind and taken prisoner by the Russians. The officers were especially hard hit.

The same night we moved back, covered by darkness and fog, to find suitable positions. We marched for several hours. Burning villages were throwing a phantom light on our retreating troops. Toward morning we crossed the Ner River near the village of Lutomiersk [Map 9c]. Beyond the river, halfway up the hills, we dug new trenches and were now facing the enemy once again. Harsher weather had set in, and the ground was frozen hard now. Our position was to the left of the village and halfway up the hill. From there we had a panoramic view: The Ner River was flowing swiftly through the valley below us; to the right there was a bridge across the river leading to the little town of Lutomiersk. Wooded hills rose in the background, interspersed by fields and meadows. That same morning we saw the Russians coming down into the valley. They arrived in single units settling along the forest's edge and in a cemetery. Our fire did not deter them from marching forward. Since we hadn't had much practice yet in the construction of trenches, ours were still very primitive. During daylight hours we were unable to work because of enemy fire so that as soon as it was getting dark we tried our best to work on our trenches. We even moved about outside the trench to limber up our stiff bodies. Still, the trenches had to remain very shallow since the soil was frozen hard; so as long as it was light we couldn't walk around in them. We were literally glued to one spot all day long in the wintery cold.

Life in a Dugout

For two full weeks we were stuck here, outdoors and in freezing weather covered with only very little straw. For myself I had dug a foxhole one meter wide into the rear wall of the trench, made myself a bench, covered it all with a board and the front with a piece of canvas. For 14 long days I was forced to sit in this prison, only at night we dared come outside. But because of my little hideaway I was at least protected somewhat against the ice-cold morning winds. A small candle lit up the space dimly, but when the mail came from home I was at least able to read it. My metal mug I hung above the light, and in it I warmed some red wine. It was extremely difficult to provide food for our company as the field kitchen had to stay far behind the lines because of the ever present danger. And when they managed to get the food safely through the firing line, once it arrived it was ice-cold. And since in the darkness we had no control over the delivery, it happened often that some groups got nothing and had to go hungry. It was just lucky that we found a barrel full of sauerkraut, as well as potatoes, which the men cooked during the night. The mornings were usually quiet. It wasn't until the sun went down and our trenches were bathed in evening sunlight that hostile artillery fire set in. Once the Russians planted a few shells right in front of me and behind me so that the earth seemed to tremble, but luck was with me, and this stormy episode passed. Other than that, the Russians kept quiet, but they did try to break through our lines to the right of us in order to take possession of a bridge across the Ner. In front of us we saw the burning town of Lutomiersk. It was a ghastly, yet strangely beautiful sight! German shrapnel was crashing into the church tower, setting it on fire so that it finally collapsed. All around us fiery blazes were flaring up.

At last we received some mail again, and so I started reading in my little underground shelter until late at night the letters from home and the latest news about the various theaters of war. My red wine mug above the candle spread a comforting glow, and momentarily I was happy as a king. How unpretentious we humans become when we find ourselves in a difficult situation, and how content with so little once we have lived through misery and privation!

The Battle Front in Late November/December 1914

By early December the Russians had initiated heavy attacks on the entire German front. On November 24, 1914, reconnaissance planes sent by our XI Corps reported a concentration of strong enemy forces in the region between Lask and Janowice [south of Lodz], as well as two columns marching against the right wing of our division. In the course of the afternoon the attack grew fiercer and fiercer, threatening to break through the German division that was fighting on a 17-kilometer front; but thanks to our strong defensive artillery fire the attack was halted.

Since we had not been able to reach Pabianice by November 19, and in the north the XI Corps had been stopped by a huge superior force, we had not been able to close the loop around Lodz. From November 22 to November 24 the situation for our troops near Brzeziny [east of Lodz] became more perilous every day, and when one evening General Litzmann saw Russian searchlights lighting up the sky from all directions, he realized that the troops under his General Scheffer were almost completely encircled, facing certain annihilation should the enemy push ahead from the west and the south. It was a stirring scene when by flickering lantern light in a small humble *Panje* house General Litzmann, the leader of the 3rd Guard-Infantry-Division, took leave from his commanding general, Freiherr von Scheffer-Boyadel. In this desperate situation both leaders promised each other with a firm handshake to fight to victory or death.

At the head of the 1st Company of the Pioneer-Battalion 28, General Litzmann with his staff would soon after storm the terrain near the railroad station of Galkow, sword in hand [see Bedon, Map 9a]. This was followed by the final blow to the Russian grip on the German army near Brzeziny [9 miles east of Lodz]. It was one of the most glorious days for our troops. No more did they have to fear an encirclement, but instead were once more attacking from a broad front which, by December 2, would include us once again. The 94th Company had already taken Hilltop 181 with its church and cemetery overlooking the Ner valley, south of Bechcice [Map 9c].

In a wild struggle with the Siberians, our troops from Thuringia broke into their position. We, too, left our trenches behind and moved forward through farmsteads, down the slope. Daylight was dimming when we arrived at the mill. Above us on the hilltop the battle raged for Hill 181. Shrapnel zoomed past us through the courtyard where our company (2nd/4, 96) was assembled, ready to attack. The wounded were coming to the mill in droves where they were given first aid. Major Brix, the leader of our 2nd Battalion, had already died a hero's death. Lieutenant Stephani was critically wounded. We were overcome by an eerie feeling on this gray December day in -10° weather [14°F] when everything looked so desolate. Inside the building one could hear the wounded moaning, and on the outside there was the whistling of shrapnel and the explosions of crashing shells. At last, when it was completely dark, it was our turn to storm ahead, first across a stream, then under cover of darkness through a narrow pass. We were getting closer and closer to the enemy fire. Machine gun fire was coming fast and furious just above our heads as we were running across an open field. Finally we recognized the highly visible cemetery cross of Hill 181. To its left was the village of Bechcice. We were soon squatting in the trench to the left of the graveyard. The battlefield was covered with corpses. There, next to the ditch, a young dead volunteer lay prone. He seemed to be slumbering peacefully. In silence we walked past in the moonlight. We were entering a farmstead, hoping to get a little rest in the farmhouse and to warm ourselves. A strange sweet odor hit us. The room was filled with limp and deformed corpses. We returned to our trench.

The battle was again in full force, a killing field. The object was to take the city of Lodz. Only a few hillsides separated us from this huge industrial complex. The Russians were trying desperately to take back the hilltop we had gained. What a pitiful sight it was to see the brave Siberians get out of their trenches only to be mowed down by our Naumburg artillery that was anchored in our trench. This battle had by now taken on large-scale proportions. The eerie play of searchlights catching with their bright beams the advancing phantomlike shapes of Russian soldiers ready to attack again and again; the thundering noise of our cannons, their explosives howling while hitting the ground with lightning flashes and sending fragments flying all over the place; the deafening rat-a-tat-tat of the machine guns and the cracking noise of the rifles —all that was like a storming, raging sea battering our ears and minds.

By next morning we had gained a firm foothold on these hills. The enemy line was broken, unable to resist any longer. When our cannons started firing again, we saw droves of fur-capped soldiers running toward us. To be sure, these brave Siberians had fought long and hard. Whoever was not dead or wounded saved himself by coming over to us. They arrived understandably frightened and hesitating, but obviously glad to save their lives in the shelter of our trenches because they were still threatened by their own guns. I saw one Siberian hit by a Russian bullet just outside our trench. A few of them were still staying behind in their trenches. But they were not able to hold on to their position, and on December 4, 1914, we were marching in extended order through the village of

Bechcice until we came upon a kiln that was hit hard by bullets. The Russians could not have withdrawn very far, for already we were being targeted by heavy artillery fire.

It was a clear, star-lit night and extremely cold, so by the time we reached the kiln in the evening, we felt frozen through and through, dead tired and half starved. Once again we had to dig trenches. Part of the company attempted to find shelter in houses; others sought refuge in the brick kiln, always under attack by heavy artillery. I entered the home of the brick-maker himself—it belonged to a German family. The rooms were empty and deserted. Blessings in German decorated the walls. The various rooms were in complete disarray. An open German catechism was lying on the table. Next to it were Christmas tree decorations from gold and silver paper evidently made by the children for the approaching Christmas season. It was heartbreaking. The family had escaped; only a dog was crouching under the bench snarling at me. Immediately I turned and walked over to the office of the brick kiln where still other officers and troops had found quarters.

An ice-cold wind was blowing through the broken window panes. We tried to cover the opening at least partially and started a fire in the tiled oven. This turned out to be a hopeless task, however, which had to be abandoned soon since the oven smoked so badly that we were suffocating in smoke in a very short time. Shivering, we lay down on the hard floor but couldn't sleep because of the cold and the noise of crashing shells. During that night I got up to join a patrol. We advanced about two kilometers. Near a farmstead I posted a field guard. The road was covered by heavy fire so that we moved away from the road (about 200 meters) to continue on a stubble field. The enemy line could not be far away. The next morning we worked our way up closer to the enemy. I went ahead with my platoon.

We have barely reached the top of a hill when we see before us a heavily fortified Russian trench. Explosives are whizzing past our ears, and black "trees" rise from the earth where shells hit the ground. One fellow next to me gets a direct hit to his head. Blood comes shooting out of his temple, a moan, and his head tilts over toward the ground. Our losses are growing. With our spades we try desperately to dig in, but the ground is hard as rock. We then try crawling back up and behind the hill on all fours, but then the game starts all over again. This time we are more successful.

By evening we had finished our trench. In a nearby farmstead we got some straw so that, at last, we were able to get an hour's sleep. We were at the end of our rope. We were completely numb and the last bit of warmth was gone from our bodies. For weeks now we had spent the nights outdoors exposed to the winter cold. We had not had any warm food the last two weeks. We had witnessed misery and death. Tonight, for the first time the field kitchen arrived with lots of steaming hot food! Right away all our misery was forgotten. One artillery officer joined me, and we were laughing and joking again over a bowl of soup and a mug of hot coffee, feeling better than ever! Only one thing was missing: the opportunity to wash ourselves. We had not been able to do so since November 14. Our hair was full of sand, and our hands and faces covered with dirt, without even mentioning our soiled clothes.

To the left of us we heard the din of battle, but all remained quiet where we were. Would we attack the enemy? This didn't seem like a good idea since the Russians were in strong, well-fortified trenches, but to our surprise, they deserted their lines the next day. Pressured by the advancing German troops, they were forced to withdraw behind the city of Lodz. So we followed them on the morning of December 6. Since we didn't know how far the Russians had retreated, we moved forward carefully in open formation. Now we saw firsthand the strong enemy entrenchments: barricades made with wire and branches, as well as wolf traps. These were so well camouflaged with twigs and moss that even in broad daylight one of my men fell through. After some time we finally reached the highest point from where, to our great surprise, we had an unexpected view: a large plain and in the background row upon row of houses, part of the city of Lodz. Once again the largest industrial city of Russian Poland was there before us, the same city we had to vacate only a little over a month earlier on October 29, 1914, and which the Russians meanwhile had re-taken. Thanks to Hindenburg's impressive offensive, we were now standing at its gates again, ready to pursue the Russians and to beat them back behind the Vistula River.

Chapter Six

THE WINTER OF 1914/15

In 1915 the war continued unabated on both fronts. However, whereas the fighting in the west turned into static trench warfare, combat on the entire Eastern Front remained fluid. Many large and smaller battles were fought there, with the result that the Russian front line was gradually pushed back by German and Austrian forces [Map 10a].

A "Second Battle of the Masurian Lakes" (the "Winter Battle") ensued in February 1915, resulting in "Hindenburg's great victory in East-Prussia," as quoted by my father.

In early March 1915, his own unit started marching again from their positions east of Lodz on the Rawka River in pursuit of the Russians. However, since my father was sent home to recuperate from a bullet wound he had sustained on this forward march, he did not return to the front until September 10, 1915.

At this time, the German high command had decided to divert troops from the Eastern Front to the west in a major effort to once again take the offensive there. Because of this repositioning, my father found himself in an officers' transport train, first heading east—then west back to France.

This chapter then begins on the Eastern Front, but ends with my father's return to the Western Front.

Holiday in Lodz

For the first time in weeks we were free from the thunderous noise of guns and of rifle fire; for the first time out of imminent danger. And for the first time we were looking forward to be able to cook, wash up, and sleep again in a *Panje* house. After an exhausting march, we reached

THE MOBILE EASTERN FRONT 1915

0   50   100
Miles

Riga

Libau
Fell on 8 May.

Memel

Dvinsk

Not captured by Germans.

Dvina

Stormed by Germans 17-18 August.

BALTIC SEA

Kovno

Germany's aim was to make the Eastern Front safe and passive so that she could switch her main assault to the Western Front (she did not hope to completely defeat Russia). Rather than instituting an "enveloping" operation, she decided to attempt a "breakthrough" attack between Gorlice and Tarnow. This commenced on 2 May 1915, in concert with the Austrians. This front contrasts sharply with the Western Front during 1915.

Königsberg

"Winter Battle" Feb. 1915

Danzig

EAST

PRUSSIA

MASURIAN LAKES

Niemen

Graudenz

Vistula

Narew

Grodno

Fell on 2 September.

RUSSIA

Thorn

Vistula

Capitulated on 20 August.

North of this position, the front line remained as shown (with minor variations) until the end of 1917.

Entered by Germans on 5 August.

Novo-Georgievsk

Warsaw

Bug

Brest-Litovsk

Pripet

Lodz

POLAND

Vistula

Surrendered on 26 August.

South of this position, the front line remained as shown (with minor variations) until June 1916.

Ivangorod

Fell on 5 August.

San

Evacuated by Russians on 22 June.

Vistula

Tarnow

Lemberg

Cracow

GALICIA

KEY

GERMAN ELEVENTH ARMY

2 MAY 1915

Przemysl

Gorlice

Fell on 3 June.

CARPATHIAN MOUNTAINS

Dniester

Pruth

Opening assault by German and Austrian armies.
Advances by German and Austrian armies.
Front line, 2 May.
Front line, 1 June.
Front line, 16 July.
Front line, 15 August.
Front line, 1 September.
Front line, winter 1915.

©Arthur Banks 1973

Tisza

Map 10a

The Mobile Eastern Front, 1915

The troops assigned to the Western Front took advantage of the excellent railroad system under German control. Rapid troop movements were the result.

Retkinia not far from Lodz in the evening of December 6, 1914, and we quartered there [Map 9c]. Oh, it felt good to drink a cup of hot tea and to eat a bowl of the familiar Knorr soup, and how wonderful it was to do something for our physical well-being, both inside and out. The next day was an entire day off. It felt like a real holiday. In an upbeat mood, we got together with our friends, and in the afternoon we took off for Lodz in a dilapidated *Panje* wagon. To get there, we had to work our way through ankle-deep mud in the suburbs. These poverty-stricken suburbs with their totally inadequate lighting were truly a sad sight. Still, it got better as we came closer to the inner city. And then after a long time, we once again saw electric streetcars and enjoyed walking past brightly lit display windows. On the whole, however, there was a great deal of poverty and need.

The "Grand Hotel" was crowded with officers, generals, and princely dignitaries. I saw among others the Grand-Duke Wilhelm Ernst von Sachsen-Weimar, the Prince and Heir Apparent Reuss, the commanding general of the XI Army Corps von Plüskow and others. The food was rather mediocre, but I made up for it with coffee and enough pancakes to satisfy my hunger.

Around ten in the evening we returned to Retkinia. We might have slept for about two hours when alarm was given. And right away the battalion was assembled on the road, ready to march. In only a few hours we were on the other side of Lodz in the suburb of Widzewo where we had quartered once before. We entered the first house we could find in order to get some more sleep. But that rest, too, was quickly interrupted. Without any morning coffee and without being able to clean up, we had to leave, crossing the railroad tracks, thus leaving the outskirts of Lodz for the second time, but this time we marched eastward. Already machine guns were beginning to bark. The tell-tale shrapnel clouds were flying through the air and between them our German pilots. The weather was dreary and foggy when we got to the village of Wioneyn Dolny just as it was getting dark. Still, we didn't get any rest. The enemy was directly in front of us, and we soon had to join another skirmishing line to extend our defensive position. The next few days went by under constant artillery duels. One evening I came to a house in order to quarter my men there. A shell had burst through the roof, killing five or six people who were now lying side by side on the floor. We had to bury the dead before being able to move into the house.

Time to Celebrate

On the evening of December 11, 1914, we were sitting in a newly fortified trench. We were there to relieve another company. For the first time I saw a primitive stove placed in a small dugout. A lieutenant who had just arrived from the west had installed it. "What luxury," we thought. We made tea and coffee to celebrate a special day, namely my birthday which would roll around at midnight. Lieutenant Grimmer contributed some *Stollen* [a traditional German Christmas bread]. And so we stayed up almost all night!

Extremely heavy shooting continued on December 13 and 14. We had experienced it all before: "shooting preceded by searchlights." Some units of our brigade were attacking. Finally, on December 17, our pilots reported the departure of Russian troops. In rainy weather, our company (2/96 Colonel Prüfer) re-united in a nearby forest, then joined the division along the road on their forward march. These roads were in indescribably poor condition; our boots got stuck in the mud and the vehicles were forced to stay far behind. At last, after a difficult march, soaked through and through by the rain, we reached a village where we spent the night in miserable, shoddy cottages. Very early the next morning we continued on our march. The weather cleared and it was freezing again. We marched on and on through vast swampy areas, and in Lachow we heard the Russians shooting once again. Finally we crossed the big country road to Rawa and came closer to the River Rylsk, marching through woods and bogs, always exposed to enemy artillery fire [Map 9a]. The battalion stayed behind in the forest while some scouting units were sent ahead first. I myself was marching toward the enemy with my platoon of the 2nd Company and Lieutenant Hoppe's platoon of the same company. We had hardly crossed the plateau and were looking down into the deep river valley when we were bombarded with heavy artillery fire. Alone and in groups, we jumped as quickly as possible down into a narrow pass offering some protection. We finally ended up above the village of Boguslawski in a deserted Russian trench, where we were certainly protected against infantry fire but where fierce artillery fire fell upon us with a vengeance and caused heavy losses. Undaunted, we proceeded, digging in as best we could after having joined forces with other units (Infantry Regiment 94) to the right and to the left .

We were now in the midst of winter. A thick blanket of snow covered the ground so that combat activities were slowing down more and more. Across from us the Russians were sitting in their primitive trenches dressed in thick heavy furcoats, while we were trying to warm our stiff limbs around our scanty fire, waiting for Christmas Eve to arrive, under these uncomfortable circumstances and so far away from home. The landscape before us appeared forlorn, desolate: a medium sized mountain range on the enemy's side with distant church towers seemingly peeking over them; a long row of pilings sticking out of the snow, marking the line of the Russian tripwire. Although this landscape appeared to be lonely and monotonous, it was not without charm. Its colors were delightful in the setting sun. The snowy fields were radiant with their red colors softening the hearts of those fighting men, as they gazed at the beauty of a sun that disappeared in the west, the home of their loved ones.

And so Christmas Eve arrived. When darkness had fallen, I climbed through the wire entanglements fronting our lines into the deserted village of Boguslawski that was also free from enemy troops. There, in one of the houses, I celebrated Christmas Eve with the youthful and spirited Lieutenant Hoppe and other fellow officers. As I was walking down into the village, this melody was softly wafting from afar across the white fields, "O du fröhliche, o du selige, gnadenbringende Weihnachtszeit" ["O thou joyful day, O thou blessed day"].

In our half-destroyed house we were not far from the enemy. We had carefully blacked out the windows toward the side of the enemy. Since there were no chairs or tables, we simply sat on a bedframe. A board in front of it served as a table. We started by singing the old familiar "Stille Nacht, heilige Nacht" ["Silent Night, Holy Night"], followed by the *Bescherung* [gift exchange]. There wasn't much by way of Christmas presents because there simply was no mail delivery, due to the miserable road conditions. (I believe it was February when we finally received our packages.) But this didn't mar our holiday spirit. A strong cup of tea and a few sweets were all we needed to make us happy and contented. Despite our wretched circumstances, we would never want to forget our Christmas in Poland, in 1914.

On December 25, 1914, I was promoted to company commander of the 2nd Company, Infantry Regiment 96. The fact that I had done my *Einjähriges* [one-year volunteer service before 1914] with the same company was a special bonus for me. There were still a number of older second lieutenants in the company that I had known before the war. From now on we were to share joy and sorrow in the field. Life on the front as a company leader marked a new beginning for me. I shared good and bad times with my company. The most rewarding task for me was to look after the welfare of my men and to make the heavy burden of life on the front a bit easier for them.

Life in the Woods

Life in the woods in our forest camp near Podkonze Duze was a pleasant interlude. We named it "Heinrichswalde" ["Henry's Woods"] in honor of our duke, Heinrich von Reuss. [Since around 1300 all male heirs

were called Heinrich, named after "Heinrich, the Russian wayfarer."] For
the first time during the war, we built a camp where we would find shelter
for a longer period of time whenever we were pulled back from the front.
Here my good musketeers worked and hammered away to build small log
cabins, as though we were meant to stay here for months. And so it was
that in a very short time a whole colony of such cabins literally grew out
of the ground, a little town in the woods, our dear Heinrichswalde. When
we weren't trenching or building, we would do field exercises. Fun and
good humor prevailed during our times off. The following poem by Second Lieutenant Standle (7/96) reflects this mood as well as describes vividly our forest home: [The complete poem is five and one-half handwritten
pages long! The translator's condensed version follows:]

> While our loved ones are anxiously awaiting news from their sol-
> dier abroad and worry about him, we are cheerfully working away,
> cutting down pine trees, hauling sand and moss with tarps, twigs and
> branches to be used as decorations for our new "colony," as if for a
> celebration. Where it was dark and solemn before amidst tall pines
> and bushes, the Polish countryside seems transformed today, airy and
> light, a friendly face welcoming the visitor, with green garlands swing-
> ing from tree to tree, sending greetings to our Germany.

> Take a good look around and see what we've done in a very
> short time: From early morning till late at night we have been clear-
> ing the woods, digging deep into the soil to make room for pine
> logs to be placed on top. To get enough straw for the roofs meant
> hiking long distances. After that we needed to cover the thatched
> roofs with lots of dirt. Of course, having this much accomplished
> we were ready to celebrate with the traditional "Richtschmaus" [to
> bless the new home with a festive meal]. Now it was time to do
> something about the cold air coming through the openings (a door
> was needed, of course) and since the walls were drafty, we quickly
> insulated them with plenty of straw. One of our corporals found a
> stove in the village and brought it back. And soon everyone was
> happily bedding down on thick layers of straw, warm and snug.
> After some rest, creative thoughts emerged, namely to transform
> old wooden boxes (from home!) into signs for streets and houses
> that read, for instance, "Bonin Street" (Bonin was one of the offic-
> ers) [Colonel von Bonin, commander of I.R. 96]. The main street
> was named after the queen, "Hindenburg" and "Ludendorff" square
> for our generals, father figure and energetic advisor respectively.
> We wanted to nourish our sense of humor and came up with names

An idyllic dugout in the woods, part of the "village" of "Heinrichswalde" ("Henry's Woods"). Observe its size and the chimney stack. The scene was sketched by F. R. Stryhan, January 21, 1915.

like "Ohnesorge" ["without worries"], "Russenburg" ["Russian Fortress"], "Russenschrecken" ["Russian Horror"], "Raubritter" ["Robber Baron"] and "Heinrichsruh" ["Henry's Repose"]. But in this cold and foggy Polish winter we were soon freezing and sneezing in our damp caves.

Yet we proudly compared our "settlement" to the resort Sülzenburg on the Elster River [a tributary of the Elbe River, northeast of Dresden]. We therefore needed gardens, if not of roses, then of greenery, such as moss, juniper, and pine. Energetically, everybody pitched in so that by evening all were looking forward to the arrival of the field kitchen with its inviting kitchen odors. Then everyone chewed away, contentedly enjoying God's gifts, wondering why man can't have two stomachs.

Although we had to do without so many things, we opened our hearts to the moment, lit a candle in the center of our cabin, the walls ringing from our boisterous laughter. Never mind sand trickling down on us or Russian bullets flying outside, we would remain true to ourselves, to our loved ones, to Kaiser and Reich! [End of summary of the poem.]

In the Trenches near the Rawka River

On January 25, 1915, our good life in the forest came to an early end. We marched to the village of Pokrywo and moved into position on the Rawka River, not far from the city of Rawa [Map 9a]. The enemy was heavily concentrated on the opposite side, and not far behind us was the Rawka River. What had once been a beautiful forest in this area was now devastated by the war; only a few tree stumps were still visible. Our dugouts were totally inadequate. Most of my men were squatting down outdoors with tarps draped over their bodies to protect themselves. It was becoming increasingly difficult to keep the trenches intact, what with loose soil slipping and crumbling. Here and there, sticking out of the parapet, we found parts of bodies, which we dug out and removed with great difficulty.

The weather in February was beautiful and the sun so warm that we were able to take off our coats. Through a telephone call on February 17 we received word of Hindenburg's great victory in East Prussia [Map 10a]. We were all in a happy mood. The nice weather lured us out into the open trench and we started shooting off salvoes, singing, and shouting "hurrah"! By way of a long pipe someone notified the Russians across from us in Polish of Hindenburg's victory, only to be rebuffed with grenades hurled at us so that we hurriedly left the danger zone.

This card picturing the trenches near the Rawka River in February 1915 was sent to Lt. R. in Rostock, Germany, where he was recuperating from a bullet wound. The card reads: "Zandlowice on the Pilica R., 5-1-15. Dear Mr. Rosenhainer. Since early April the 96th I.R. occupies a great position near the Pilica River. Weather is also great. Gradually, our fellow officers are all returning. At present, we are four or five officers in our company. All is well, Love, A. Petzold." This card is addressed to: His Highness, Res. Lt. Rosenhainer. ROSTOCK, KaiserWilhelmstr. 14. Field Postal Service. It is stamped: 5-3-15 3-4N K. O. Field Postal Service XO of the Division Menges.

On the whole, not too much fighting went on; there was only weak artillery fire, and mines were thrown from both sides. Life in the trenches near the Rawka River was a lot more tolerable now that it was nice and warm outside. However, in early March the weather changed. It became bitter cold again and a thick blanket of snow covered the ground. One evening the company commanders of the 1st Company (Colonel Lategahn) and the 2nd Company (Lieutenant Rosenhainer) were asked to see the battalion commander. We were told that we were to take part in a larger offensive against the Russians.

Renewed Pursuit of the Russians

On March 3, 1915, we started marching in deep snow. Early in the morning I walked with the company commander of the 1st Company, Colonel Lategahn, through marshes to Pokrzywo. It had already been getting light without our realizing it, but they were shooting at us off and on. Our companies arrived in the evening, and we marched straight to Linkow where we had something to eat from our field kitchen. We had a lovely time in the quarters of our chaplain (Pastor Stüber), reviving old memories and discussing heatedly coming events. Where would we attack? How long would our campaign last? We were then marching throughout the night on godforsaken roads with harsh, cold winds blowing from the east. The snow made a crunching sound under our feet, and it was nearly impossible to detect any trail underneath the white cover of snow. Our men were stomping through the deep snow like a group of polar voyagers. My feet were so ice-cold that I jumped from my horse and led it by its bridle in order to get my circulation going and get warm again. At long last, after a tiring night march, we reached a village where we stopped for a short rest. The field kitchens arrived and a mug of steaming coffee was warming our bodies a bit before we continued our march via Gluchow, until early morning. Several of our men couldn't keep up the pace, but in the end everybody made it and found some peace and warmth in the *Panje* homes of the village of Zelechlin. But here, too, our stay was short. Once again we were getting close to the enemy lines, near Bechcice. We got another night's rest before the scheduled assault.

New batteries, German and Austrian, were already being assembled but were still quiet and looked threatening in their positions, as we were marching toward the enemy at dusk on March 5, 1915. Then our barrage set in, a few shots at first, then more frequently and getting stronger and stronger. Shots were pitching, howling, and whirling through the air to end up in the enemy's trenches with a thunderous noise. Then a few batteries

Lt. R. as company commander of the 2nd Company in the trenches near the Rawka River, March 1915.

of our field artillery came up close and opened fire. We stood assault-ready in the second line. The first line attacked and took possession of the first trenches. For hours we waited in a wooded area, exposed to bitter cold, frost-bitten and hungry. At last, towards evening, we were told to push forward. At about that time, an endless stream of wounded coming from up front passed us, many moaning and groaning, others serene and obviously not in pain, some on crutches moving forward with difficulty, while others were being carried blood-soaked on tarps. The woods echoed from falling Russian shrapnel, and whistling infantry bullets hit the trees and the ground. By evening we had reached the other side of the forest. Trying to get across a trench, I stumbled over two corpses that were mangled miserably. On the parapet sat a young soldier who had lost one eye. I helped him bandage the wound, and he walked back with a grateful smile. Before me I saw corpse after corpse, almost all Germans. They were bleeding from a thousand wounds; many had suffered head wounds. Severely wounded men were lying everywhere, lying outdoors in -15° [8° F] temperature and pleading with us for just a little water and help in getting them out of there. Our hearts were aching in the face of so much suffering, yet there was nothing we could do to help them. We kept running, running into the dark night. Shells were flying all around us. Empty fields surrounded us. We were on a vast snow-covered plateau across which a fierce cold wind was blowing.

We come to an old Russian trench and we jump in to seek shelter from the wind and get some rest. I see someone sitting next to me. I touch him and notice that it is a dead Russian soldier. We throw the corpse out of the trench and try to get some sleep. But we can't help shivering from the cold, and, unable to rest, we jump across the parapet and move about to warm our limbs a bit. At long last it's morning. Stiff from the cold, frozen to the bone, we advance again in open formation. The Russians have retired further, and we are finally collecting our men in a small forest to await new orders. Since we are so fatigued and worn out, we crawl into abandoned Russian dugouts and light a small fire.

At dusk we reached the village of Sandborz via Straska. That's as far as we got because the Russians were occupying strong positions in the woods across from us and had started shooting again with their artillery. We had no choice but to dig into the hard frozen ground and to construct new trenches along the perimeter of the village. The place had been deserted by the villagers and was almost completely destroyed, so there was no way to find warm overnight quarters. During the night we finished the new trenches. Needless to say, the Russians, having noticed our entrenchments, began to immediately bombard Sandborz and the village of Rudki next to it. This resulted in heavy losses and affected my company, too. There was a house with two rooms in the middle of our line. We walked into the large room to get warm and to cook something. Two men were asleep in the smaller room next to ours. Lieutenants Petzold and Günther and myself were just having a cup of coffee when suddenly there was a big bang! A dud had crashed into the next room, killing both men. As we were lifting the tarp from them we saw one (Grötsch) completely torn apart and the other one with two smashed legs. A number of shells had come down in the village, killing several men in one of the dugouts. The cold weather continued and we had to remain in this location for several days. We therefore decided to take turns staying one night in the village, and the next night in the trench on the edge of town, until we were finally given the signal to march forward. Our regiment was on the move again, and we were told to entrench near Grabice [Map 9a]. The frost subsided and with warmer temperatures the roads became once again mud-clogged.

Wounded near Grabice

After having been quartered in shoddy, crumbling huts we were to move into new positions on March 16, 1915. It was already broad daylight when we got the orders. I therefore led my company carefully in wide, open formation. It wasn't long before the Russian artillery started shooting. It was as though sprinkling cans were pouring shrapnel onto the fields while we were trying hard to reach the woods. Suddenly I feel something hitting me hard. I grab my chest before noticing blood squirting out of my leggings on my left shinbone. I am hitting the ground. The troops are racing double-quick across the fields, above which bursts of shrapnel are still dancing wildly. Despite it all, I succeed in reaching the forest's edge where I am safe. A munition wagon happens to be leaving just then and they are taking me to the field dressing station where soon after and having etherized me briefly, the medical officer, laughing, holds up a bullet for me to see!

The field dressing station is a miserable Polish peasant hut whose broken window panes have been taped over; makeshift bedding on the floor. There is a great deal of commotion in the room, a constant coming and going. They are bringing in the wounded; others are being taken away. There is simply no space left in the place. A sergeant is lying there. He was shot in the stomach and seriously wounded. All night he is moaning and whimpering until, suddenly, he turns over from pain and his crying stops. The stretcher-bearers are carrying him out the next morning.

Next to me lies another soldier, seriously wounded. His cheeks are flushed from a fever, but now he seems to be sleeping. The orderly comes and throws a blanket over his face. They are taking him away, too.

Later a motor ambulance took me to a field hospital in Tomaszow on the Pilica River [Map 9a], where we were well taken care of by Catholic Sisters until, finally, a hospital train transported me to a military hospital in Frohnau near Berlin. That marked the end of the first part of my life on the front.

Interlude: Repositioning of Troops

On September 10, 1915, at 9:15 a.m., we traveled by train from Gera (Reuss) to Weimar. This included Lieutenants Tritschler, Fasshauer, Fritsche, Ensign Kammann and Orderly Neumann. In Weimar an officer transport train, eastward bound, was waiting for us: four officers from the 96th Regiment, one from the 71st, two from the 95th, and five from the 94th. On the evening of September 10 we arrived in Berlin. The next day we traveled east via Frankfurt (on the Oder River), Posen, Thorn, Osterode to Allenstein [East Prussia].

It is a gorgeous September day. Near Thorn we see again the first signs of war: rows of barbed wire, fortifications of all kinds, even more near Ortelsburg. Of interest are large log cabins, built fairly close together, from where the entire area can be covered by machine gunners. Strong wire defenses run along the railroad tracks. We spend the second night in beautiful Allenstein and continue traveling on September 12 by way of Johannisburg, Dlottowen to Kolno [Map 4]. As soon as we cross the border we notice a typically neglected landscape. The fields, for the most part, are left uncultivated. In the border town of Kolno we see the vast depot of this railroad hub and in the center of town the beautiful church. Since they have moved the general headquarters from Kolno to Bialystock, we are forced to choose an alternate route by traveling back to Johannisburg. It is difficult to find quarters here, all hotels are closed, but finally we get settled in a field hospital. Numerous fire-bombed ruins in the city are testimony to the time the Russians had been here. In Lyck, too, where we arrive on September 12, we find a large church and the railroad station completely destroyed. We are well taken care of in the "Hotel Königlicher Hof" ["Hotel Royal Court"] and enjoy the beautiful fall weather while walking along the lake. The next day, on September 13, we again cross the border near Prosten-Grajewo. The entire next day is spent on the train. At one station, Ruda, the train stops for hours. Here the people have all left the village, and by now our *Landstürmer* [special infantry unit] have beautified the place

Lt. R. wrote on the back of this photo: "Sept. 10, 1915. Departure from Gera. Rosenhainer, wearing a coat, second from right."

with lovely gardens and nice little porches and verandas. Military cemeteries are a reminder of the fighting that took place here. Otherwise, the town is surrounded by a cheerless desertlike stretch of sand and occasional pine forests.

Late that evening the train started rolling again. Several troop transport trains were allowed to pass through before us. On the morning of September 15, we came to Bialystok [today's Belostok], where numerous units were arriving ready for transport. At the break of dawn, we stood shivering on the loading ramp, then proceeded to walk into the town which left us with a rather bad impression, the

Lt. R. points out the "fire-bombed ruins" in the city of Johannisburg (in East Prussia).

dismal streets dragging on cold and bare. The railroad station and the surrounding buildings had been burnt to the ground by the Russians. Beams, rubble, cables, railroad tracks were strewn about pell-mell, but Russian prisoners were already at work to clean up the tangled mess. Aside from the ancient Polish castle there were very few attractive buildings in Bialystok. We tried to find some nice stores, but in vain, although a lot of bartering was going on. There is quite a large Jewish population here, too, enlivening the street scene with their caftans. Communication was relatively easy since most Jews understand German. In addition, quite a number of Germans live here. In business letters, for instance, we also noticed the German language in addition to Russian and Polish. The administrative arm of the military had seen to it that German street names were also affixed to the old ones. The streets were crowded with German columns of all kind: cars, ambulances, ammunition wagons, food supply vehicles, artillery, and so on.

On September 17, we still didn't know where our regiment was stationed, since a large scale repositioning of troops was taking place. We sent a telegram to headquarters and were waiting for an answer. We ordered two *Panje* wagons for our luggage, just in case, for there was no train connection to Grodno as yet, which meant we would have to walk. For the time being we found quarters in the Kasan barracks. The modern

Wagon supply trains moving through Bialystock, Russian Poland, on September 15, 1915.

buildings were in good condition, built around a large square. Troop trans-
ports were coming and going endlessly. These barracks were just being
readied for the German army. Everywhere you looked they were scrub-
bing floors, painting, and fixing electric lights.

Finally, on the evening of September 17, a telegram arrived from
army headquarters ordering us to go to Grodno as soon as we had received our food supplies. Since we had trouble getting enough vehicles, an
effort complicated by the fact that this was a Jewish holiday, we decided to
travel by train rather than continue on foot. It would take us back to
Lyck. From there we would get to Grodno (via Markgrabowa-Suwalki).
On September 18 the weather was cold and it was raining. Huge amounts
of war materials and horses were being loaded onto trains. Shivering, we
took seats in a second class compartment after having disposed of our
luggage, which proved to be difficult as usual. The train was winding its
way via Ossowez toward the border through marshlands that were heavily
fortified by the Russians. Towards morning around four o'clock we were
back in Lyck. There were a great many officers, all of them trying to get
back to the theater of war. Because of troop dispositions, we had to lay
over again in a small East Prussian village (Kruglanken) and wait for
some train to pick us up. So a veritable caravan of officers, troops and
civilians was descending upon the inn, naturally resulting in considerable
pushing and shoving. Around six o'clock, we departed for Markgrabowa.
We arrived there after long hours of traveling in overcrowded compart-
ments and were lucky that there was room for us at the "Kronprinzen
Hotel" [Crownprince Hotel].

On September 20 we reached Suwalki in a troop transport train.
Here, too, we were noticing huge installations ordered by the German
military administration. The city seemed rather dreary as we left the railroad station. But the downtown area looked a lot friendlier, especially
since the Germans had worked to clean it up. The Hotel "Frank" we were
assigned to defied description. By German standards, it was definitely
more like a hostel than a hotel and dirty beyond words. We had to coax
them into changing the dirty bed linens for us. And yet, their prices were
pretty steep. We were glad to be able to leave this place the next day. We
had been quite cold during the night with little to cover us and bothered
by steel springs poking our bodies. Far from well rested, we started walking to the depot.

The train was scheduled to leave for Augustowo at 11:45 a.m., but
we had to wait around until 8 p.m. before the seemingly endless train
finally started moving. This September night had turned quite chilly so

that we wrapped our blankets around us. Gradually the slow, rocking motion of the train lulled us to sleep. Then another sudden stop and layover in the midst of a pine forest, from midnight until eight o'clock the next morning. A radiant sun came up and after a cup of coffee (made in a cooking hole in the ground), we were finally wide awake. At last we were rolling again! But repeated stops followed. Ammunition trains had the right of way! When would we finally reach our destination? Reports came through from general headquarters that Vilna had been taken. We therefore thought that our regiment was already up front again.

Around 10 a.m. we arrived in Augustowo [Map: inside back cover]. The area where we had come through looked very much like our lake region in Meeklenburg. There, glistening lakes are visible through the vast pine forests. Augustowo, too, has a lovely location. But how little use has been made of it! There are no beautiful gardens or villas to enhance the character of the landscape, only sub-standard houses along nondescript streets. On the country road leading to Augustowo automobile traffic was quite heavy. Large groups of wounded were taken to the railroad station. By two o'clock we succeeded in catching one of the ambulance cars that would take us to Grodno. At full speed the ambulance wound its way through long columns of vehicles all the way to Grodno, where we arrived in the late afternoon.

The trip was very interesting. First we drove through the beautiful lake region of Augustowo and its forest. Here we saw the rather heavy Russian fortifications becoming more and more massive, the closer we got to Grodno. The towering church cupolas of the city were welcoming us from afar, glowing in the evening sun. Finally we entered the deeply carved valley of the Njemen River. On top of a steep hill were the large buildings of this fortified city. The railroad bridge that used to connect the two sides of the river at dizzying heights, now lay in shambles in the river below. The city itself made a much better impression than any of the Russian cities I had seen up to now. Lovely squares in parklike settings and rather narrow, winding streets. We reported to the division and were welcomed with tea and open-faced sandwiches. The city was filled with troops. That's why we had to find quarters on our own, which we finally accomplished after a long search. We stayed with a supply sergeant. We did have to sleep on the bare floor, but were glad to at least have a roof over our heads.

On September 23 we are on the lookout for a wagon, but instead I run into a side-car from our I/96 [the author's infantry unit]. They will take my luggage to wherever the I/96 is quartered. We now learn that

In Grodno, Russia: Greek Orthodox church, towering in the background. Red Cross wagon in the foreground. These letters and numbers are visible on the original photo: FL12 XV AK KW.

our regiment is being pulled back, but no one knows where they are going. Another two-hour trip through a beautiful, hilly landscape and I finally reach the village Mitzkjewitschi, where I assume command of the
3rd Company, Infantry Regiment 96. On September 25, 1915, on a beautiful, sunny autumn day and after a long ride (on horseback) through
beautiful forests, we once again reach Augustowo.

We quartered in the Cossack barracks near the railroad station. In
the evening the officers of the regiment dined in the officers' mess-hall
of Augustowo. On September 26, 1915, departure for Kosowka. It was a
very strenuous march through an area with forests and lakes. The roads
were in good condition for a change. At the border town of Prosken the
whole battalion was deloused; that is, in huge installations our clothes
and everything we had with us went through a special cleansing process
and made bug free. And our men themselves took showers. After that we
sat around in bath robes for hours in one of the recreation rooms. Late in
the evening we left Prosken, traveling by train via Lyck-Allenstein-
Schneidemühl to Berlin-Aachen-Namur and finally arrived in Douai
[France].

Chapter Seven

FRANCE, 1915–1916: THE BATTLE OF VERDUN

Belgium Revisited

The trip through Belgium was very interesting for us. The numerous mines and factories reflected the country's large industrial base. Starting with Andenne we came through familiar territory. Last year in August our victorious troops were marching through the burning town where heavy fighting had just taken place. The fire-gutted houses remain. Yet already everything looked friendlier, once again. Then we came through the valley near Namur, into which we had descended during heavy fighting on August 23, 1914. Up there on the citadel's mountain we saw the castle in ruins, the same one that had gone up in flames that August day, bombarded by German explosives. Now the tower of a radio station was visible there. We spent several pleasant hours in Douai, a pretty French town of medium size. Crowds of German troops were milling about. At this time the French had already planned and carried out their fall offensive of 1915 in the Champagne and Artois provinces. However, the French-English attack did not end in a decisive victory. The breach into the German lines was only 3 kilometers deep and 13 kilometers wide. Then, in mid-October, the attack was weakening and did not succeed in breaking through the line. This meant that our own division was no longer needed.

One evening we suddenly departed, marching throughout the night as far as Wallers. This industrial and coal-rich area is rather flat and monotonous. One little town follows another. Coal piles form pointed hills that protrude from the plain. The homes are for the most part rather modest in appearance, but inside they are much nicer than you would expect. Behind the houses is usually a well-tended vegetable garden. Under the

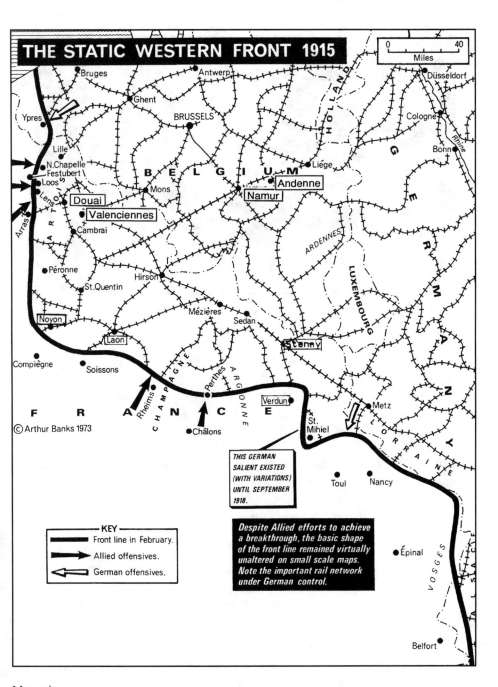

THE STATIC WESTERN FRONT 1915

0   40
Miles

Bruges

Antwerp

Düsseldorf

Ghent

BRUSSELS

Cologne

Ypres

HOLLAND

Lille

Bonn

N.Chapelle

Liége

G

Festubert

Loos

B E L G I U M

Andenne

E

Douai

Mons

Namur

Lens

ARTOIS

Valenciennes

Arras

Cambrai

ARDENNES

R

Péronne

LUXEMBOURG

M

St.Quentin

Hirson

Mézières

Noyon

Sedan

A

Laon

Stenay

Compiègne

Soissons

N

Z

CHAMPAGNE

Rheims

Perthes

ARGONNE

Verdun

Metz

F   R   A   N   C   E

St.
Mihiel

LORRAINE

© Arthur Banks 1973

Châlons

**THIS GERMAN
SALIENT EXISTED
(WITH VARIATIONS)
UNTIL SEPTEMBER
1918.**

Toul

Nancy

**Despite Allied efforts to achieve
a breakthrough, the basic shape
of the front line remained virtually
unaltered on small scale maps.
Note the important rail network
under German control.**

Épinal

VOSGES

ALSACE

Belfort

KEY

—————— Front line in February.

➤ Allied offensives.

⟵ German offensives.

Map 10b

The Static Western Front, 1915

In Noyon, France (Map 10b). Caption reads: "506. German troops in one of the streets in Noyon. Cathedral in background." Notice boarded-up front windows.

circumstances, the people have little choice but to be friendly towards us. The man in the street says, *"Ce sont les capitalistes qui ont fait la guerre"* ["This war is all the fault of the capitalists"]. For the rest, they do not hide their firm belief in a French military victory.

On the evening of October 8, 1915, we travelled from Wallers via Valenciennes to Noyon where we arrived late at night after a short march [Map 10b]. Because the front was so close by, the city was blacked out and it was difficult for us to find our quarters. This old town with its friendly old buildings and the magnificent city hall was very impressive. It was filled with German troops. We were to replace the IX A.K. [Army Corps] in their positions.

Reports from the theaters of war: The French offensive has been stopped. In the Balkans, Bulgaria attacks, and German and Austrian forces have crossed the Danube and the San Rivers to invade Bulgaria. [Bulgaria had entered the war on the side of the Central Powers on October 12, 1915.]

A Different Kind of Trenches

At dawn on October 10, I ride on horseback, along with the battalion's staff, to the positions on the front. We come through the lovely valley of the Oise River, at times through the most beautiful beech forests, then pass the Palais Ourscamp where the regiment's staff is quartered. We take a short break at this imposing structure (unfortunately heavily damaged in

Caption reads: "Soldiers shopping at the weekly market in Noyon." Here, too, all windows are shuttered or boarded up.

part), before moving on past the military cemetery that puts us in a thoughtful mood. We come to the regimental camp. Light rifle fire tells us the entrenchments are nearby. The guards are expecting us. They warn us to be aware of certain dangerous communication trenches and point out the safe ones on the way to the front. It's not easy to find your way through the maze of trenches and it takes good judgment. A veritable labyrinth of trenches is opening up before us. We walk past many a perfect hide-away along the wall of the palace gardens, then through the old park. Numerous shell holes in the walls and several soldiers' graves tell of the battles that have taken place here. The picturesque bridge across the pond in the park has partly collapsed, but the water diverted from the mill stream rushes by just as noisily. And the little make-shift bridge that our combat engineers have made from birch trees looks ever so attractive under a canopy of golden autumn leaves. Before us is the small palace of Bailly, heavily damaged by gunfire. The entire roof has collapsed with only the massive side walls left standing. Next to it a number of German and French soldiers have found their eternal rest. The graves have been lovingly enclosed with small fences and marked with wooden crosses. Most of them show the names of the dead soldiers but on some we read, "Resting place of an unknown German hero," or "Resting place of two brave, unknown French soldiers." There is nothing but death and devastation, and now a solemn silence under the autumn sun.

We now come to the area's observation post. A guard is trying to spot the enemy through a periscope, but all is quiet. It's morning and our men are bathing in the creek. The supervising corporal makes his report, then everything proceeds as planned.

I manage to zig-zag forward through a deep communication trench. I am in the line of fire where the trench narrows and is re-enforced with fascines ["fascines" are bundles of faggots]. Covered by armored shields or looking through periscopes, individual guards stand there observing the enemy. They must not open the shutters too far or, right away, there will be a well-aimed shot from the other side. By day it would be foolhardy to try to

The small palace of Bailly, heavily damaged by gunfire.

peer across the parapet, that is, above the trench. Everything in the trench is extremely neat, no paper or cartridge-cases on the floor. Each trench has its own name and sign-post to show the way. Despite it all we often get lost, especially at night. Therefore, in case of an alarm every soldier must know his exact spot where a small sign is placed with his name on it, and he must be able to find it even when it is pitch dark. All rifles are in ship-shape condition and kept in bullet-proof closets. The machine guns are also stashed away safely so they won't be damaged by artillery fire, but at night they are set up for combat. This applies also to the search-light: It can be activated within two minutes.

However, we are eager to see more. By night we steal across the big sap trench, all the way to the barbed wire maze up front. The enemy seems to have noticed us. A star shell shoots up into the air with a hissing sound right away and bullets begin whistling around our heads. We duck down deep into the trench until the small parachute of the French star shell has landed on the ground. At the end of the trench we notice a small flickering light. It's coming from the dugout of the corporal who is on guard duty up front, along with eight men. I am entering a nice little room where a few of our men are busy reading. The corporal takes me up

Photo A   Photo B

With much care a well-fortified system of trenches was put in place in the Bailly (Noyon) area. Notice in photo a) the tiled floor and gutter, with the author and his orderly standing next to a signpost that reads: "Third Company Commander." In his lapel he wears the ribbon of the Iron Cross, 2nd Class. Photo c) shows Lt. R. peeking out the window, his orderly next to him in the doorway. Heavy oak logs were used to fortify this dugout.

Photo C   Photo D

front even further. Crouching low, he leads me into a sap trench in which we can walk upright after a few steps. We are now very close to the enemy's trench. A little light comes through a few loopholes. A few dark figures are on guard duty at this dangerous outpost.

Our time at Bailly, near Noyon, was not marked by a lot of fighting, yet we suffered quite a few losses during this time. The peaceful cemetery in the forest near Ourscamp tells the story [see photo in front matter]. On October 18, 1915, we had our first wounded in France. The telephone operator gave me this report, "Herr Leutnant, at 2:15 our heavy artillery will start shooting." Soon the big shells were landing on the other side, causing earth and wooden planks to shoot upwards. The French weren't far behind with their answer and soon the earth reverberated from incoming shells. A sergeant comes running, "Herr Leutnant. Three of our men have been wounded by shrapnel splinters; one of them seriously." Quickly I run to the rear. All three have already been bandaged. One has lost his hearing, the other seems to have been luckier: His wounds are on his arm and on both legs. The third lies prone on the stretcher, moaning pitifully.

We made good use of our time by building new dugouts and by repairing damaged and collapsed parts of the trench system. We had little free time. It was a nice change of pace for me to take part in a special training course for company commanders in Cuts near Carleport, where cavalry men instructed us also in the more advanced skills of horseback riding. And once I was sent on a special mission to the 94th Regiment near Moulin-sous-Touvent. This is the area where there are vast caves with subterranean passageways of gigantic proportions, where one could have easily hidden entire divisions, complete with their vehicles.

Under Gas Attack

In Moulin-sous-Touvent I moved with my orderly into a dugout in the second line of the entrenchments. We had just fallen into a deep sleep when someone knocked at the door shouting, "Gas alarm!" I thought it was just an exercise, but already a strong odor was permeating our dugout.

We quickly put on our gas masks and run outside. It is pitch dark. Impeded by his gas mask, the battalion commander is groping his way to the telephone dugout. And now there are thick gray layers of fog descending upon this low-lying area while the French artillery is covering the entire trench area with heavy artillery fire. The shell fragments fly hissing and whining above our heads since the trench is situated in the lee of a hillside. Our gas masks have done their job. The machine guns and

Company commanders received special training in the advanced skills of horseback riding in Cuts near Carleport. Lt. R. is third from right.

Entrance to the "Adolf-Friedrich" Cave. Adolf-Friedrich VI was the last reigning grand duke of Mecklenburg-Strelitz. The left plaque shows the grand duke's personal coat-of-arms. His initials are super-imposed on the stripes of possibly the Mecklenburg flag. The plaque next to it probably represents the imperial coat-of-arms. The small sign to the right of the standing soldier reads: "8th Company, (?) Mecklenburg Grenadier Regt. No. 89." Scroll on wall, *lower right*, appears to express a friendly welcome. (Records indicate that the grand duke paid official visits to his regiment from time to time.) On the back of the card Lt. R. refers to this cave erroneously as the "Strelitz" Cave which was located nearby.

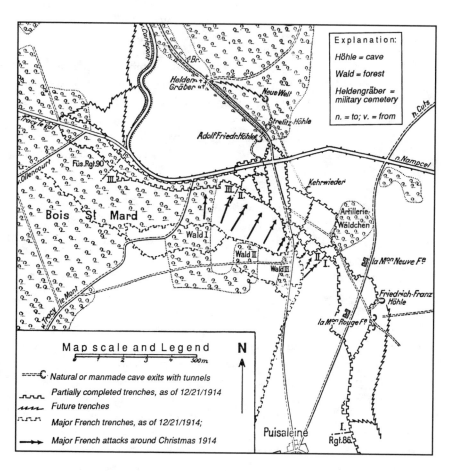

Explanation:

Höhle = cave

Wald = forest

Heldengräber = military cemetery

n. = to; v. = from

Map scale and Legend

N

0 1 2 3 4 500m

═══C· Natural or manmade cave exits with tunnels

Partially completed trenches, as of 12/21/1914

Future trenches

Major French trenches, as of 12/21/1914;

Major French attacks around Christmas 1914

"Cave Map" for Picture (on previous page)

The upper part of the map shows the entrance to the "Adolf-Friedrich" Cave with a tunnel leading to the Strelitz Cave.

all other defensive weapons have remained intact so that the French attack is halted from the start.

Having been in the center of a theater of war for months, the town
of Moulin-sous-Touvent was practically leveled. Hardly a wall was left
standing. All winter long and into May we remained in the Bailly entrenchments. It turned out to be a dreary, rainy winter.

Christmas, 1915

For the second time we men in uniform celebrate Christmas in enemy territory. It simply doesn't feel like Christmas in this kind of weather.
Rain, nothing but rain. The trenches gradually turn into watery ditches,
and the company commander is forever trying to figure out how and
where to divert all that water. The dirt, reinforced with boards and fascines,
comes loose, due to its soggy weight, and forms regular barriers across
the trench. That means we have to take hoes and spades and try to stabilize the trench walls, again and again. In the dugouts the ground water is
slowly rising from below, across the floors; and there is rain water drip-
ping down from above which we are trying to catch in a tarp. Nothing is
safe from the rats. They devour the bread along with the backpack and at
night they flit across our covers.

But what do we care on this Christmas Eve? A blanket of silence is
covering the trenches but inside, the dugouts are coming alive. To celebrate Christmas, anybody who doesn't have to be on guard duty has
come down into the dugout where the Christmas tree is lit, and the presents from home are ready to be distributed. This Christmas celebration
is much more pleasant than the one in Russia in 1914. The walls of the
dugouts are all made with boards, sometimes even wallpapered. There is
a real stove and there are even a few pieces of furniture. The candles are
burning and everyone joins in singing, "Oh, how joyful..." We all stay and
have a good time together until midnight. It is the same in every dugout,
and again on New Year's Eve. Of course, we don't celebrate it here as
exuberantly as we sometimes do in times of peace; most of us are serious
and contemplative. A song can be heard here and there along the trench.
Two older soldiers are even humming the "Wacht am Rhein" ["Watch on
the Rhine"], which shows us that the good old spirit is still alive.

In these trenches we suffer greatly from the wet conditions. Even
under normal conditions the Oise River valley is swampy with a water
level less than one meter below the ground. It is therefore out of the
question to build technically adequate emplacements. All construction must
be done in part above ground and must be covered by several layers of
beams that, naturally, offer no protection against heavier caliber shells.

Photo A

Photo B

More Bailly entrenchments. The sign above the entrance in photo b) reads: "Dugout of the company commander of the Middle Company." The soldier on the right is holding a cat in his arms. Heavy log construction is visible in photo c). One log is being cut to be put to use.

Photo C

The author's note on the back of this photo reads: "Lt. Trabert in his dugout (under construction). April 16, Bailly."

What an enormous amount of work was involved in getting the heavy oak logs to the trenches! They had to be dragged across the trenches at night under infantry and artillery fire. Later on we started building with concrete, which worked out just great and which offered the utmost protection. Granted, we had taken over many of the older structures from the Hanseatic and the Mecklenburg regiments, but many of these proved to be too weak against stronger fire power; many in fact had crumbled in the course of time. So we were never without work during those long winter months.

Quiet Life in the Noyon Area during the Winter Months

Gradually we felt quite at home in our entrenchments. The beautiful countryside added to that feeling. Is there a more beautiful view for the nature lover than the one from the "Sellert Trail" onto the wooded hills of Tracy-le-Val? And how indescribably beautiful is a walk past the small palace of Bailly, through the Reussengraben [Moat of Reuss] along the Wasserrattenweg [Waterrat Trail] into the park of the Quenotterie. To be sure, the beautiful old palace is heavily damaged from artillery fire and is about to collapse. For a little diversion I sometimes ride with my fellow officers to Ourscamp. Each time we admire the old palace, with the picturesque ruins of its abbey and the church that has remained intact. The spinning-mill on the palace grounds has been completely destroyed by the battles that have taken place here. How much prosperity, happiness, and peaceful comfort have been lost! The gardens are still being maintained by our soldiers and many a fresh vegetable improves our fare.

The Germans have made themselves at home in Ourscamp. Several groups of staff officers are quartered in this palace. They have opened up a regular bathhouse, and a "Reuss Theater at the Front" has opened its doors. For this they are using a former factory hall. It is remarkable what

Lt. R. wrote on the reverse side of this photo: "Entrance to the castle of Ourscamp on the Oise River."

our men turned actors have been able to accomplish. In addition, the hall is used as a reading room. On opening night I saw the play, "Europa in Flammen" ["Europe in Flames"], an episode in a U-boat during the war. But other plays are performed also, such as the "Spanische Fliege" ["Spanish Fly"]. This is truly a wonderful distraction for the soldiers at the front.

Once you stepped outside Ourscamp you saw the picturesque old city of Noyon in the distance. The Oise River, which winds its way through the valley, turned into a wild stream in the springtime. We continued through the forest, once a haven for deer, through Sempigny and Pont-l'Evêque toward Noyon. Magnificent the old cathedral and above all the city hall. Next to it on the market place was the German Officers' Club. Here we felt halfway civilized. They served us beer and something to eat in very com-

fortable surroundings. Whatever kind of military unit was in the vicinity gathered here: the guard corps, a *Landwehr* division and our 38th Division. There was a constant coming and going in the market place since there were several German stores, including a bookstore run by the military, where we could buy the latest books and newspapers.

During the entire period we stayed in this area our own combat activity was relatively calm, only the French artillery fire was frequently very heavy. They often surprised us with a sudden barrage of fire, forcing us to fling ourselves flat against the trench wall. We frequently sent out reconnaissance patrols. Sometimes we engaged in field exercises behind the front line and practiced throwing hand grenades

This is an unusual grave of a German soldier buried in France; well maintained, with a beautiful, carved stone in an idyllic setting. The inscription is as follows: "Ensign Rust. 1st Kp. Pion. Bat. L Nr. 9. Died 23 Nov., 1914."

In May 1916, these troops were quartered in Monceau, France (Lt. R. in foreground, center). *To the right*, between the trees, one can see a band performing. One villager, *to the left*, has joined the troops.

Lt. R. on horseback. He wrote on the back: "Monceau, France. May 1916."

Lt. R. in Monceau.

in preparation for the fighting ahead. Finally, the day of our departure arrived. We felt spring's arrival everywhere. With a magic hand it had produced the most luscious green. In the park, violets and other spring flowers were already in bloom. Forested areas stretched across the landscape like huge, green ribbons. The troops had already started building summer arbors.

It was a mild spring night when we finally had to leave our trenches. It was not so easy to do. One more time we celebrated in our new concrete dugout which had just been completed. How much labor and love had gone into finishing these trenches; how much hard work by the sweat of our brow. But also a lot of blood. The relief troops arrived, and we handed over equipment, maps, and sketches. We took a last look at our homy shelter, at the old dugout vault of a kitchen and marched off along our "house" and "park" lanes.

A gentle rain was coming down and one could literally feel buds swelling and leaves and blossoms bursting open. We had by now left the old life behind us and something new and unknown loomed ahead. How fortunate that we didn't know it. But for now, at least, we were away from the front line. Once again, we were able to raise our heads without fear, while the rifle fire became weaker and weaker. The next day, after a march of several hours, we arrived in a hamlet on the Oise River. Our friendly host, an artillery officer, welcomed us in a beautiful villa and soon we fell into a deep sleep after the exertions of the past night. We didn't stay long in our quiet quarters. In fact, we were on our way the very next day, through the beautiful valley of the Oise River, to board our train. Where this journey would take us no one knew. The word was that we were to remain on hold for a longer period behind the front lines. That meant we were headed in the direction of Laon [Map 10b]. For a few days we stayed in the village of Monceau where we had practice drills. No one worked too hard at it. I guess, the main objective was for the division to get plenty of rest. Once the regiment's band even played happy marches and tunes on the village square. Then one day we received orders: Mock attacks on fortified field positions are to be practiced at utmost speed!

The Battle of Verdun, May 1916

It wasn't long before we boarded our train to Verdun. In the vicinity of Stenay, the headquarters of the crown prince, we got off again and settled in rather squalid quarters. For a few days we engaged in military exercises and did trial runs in taking over the nearby hills above the Maas River. Old, deserted trenches and grave after grave above, on the edge of the forest, told the story. We finally learned that it would be our

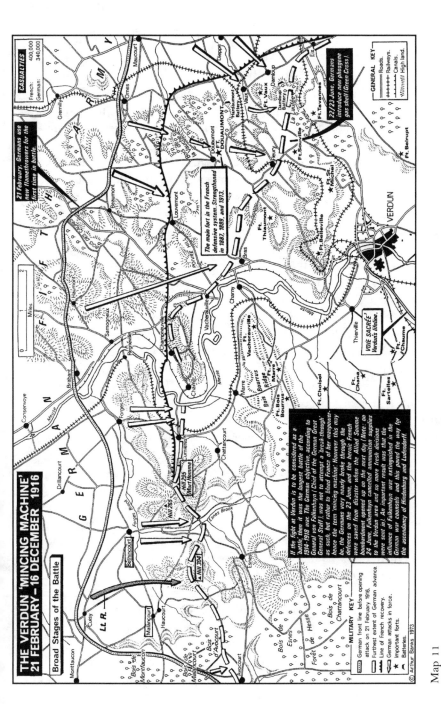

Map 11

The Verdun Mincing Machine

In May 1916 Lt. R. and his regiment approached the battle zone of Verdun from the northwest toward Hill 304.

job to attack the trenches on Hill 304 near Verdun. Once again we were
taken a little closer to the fort. For three days we had to bivouac in the
vicinity of Brieuilles. Unfortunately, a steady rain set in just then, which
didn't stop until three days later when we resumed our march. All roads
had turned into an incredible morass. Water seeped into the tents so that
it was soon impossible to find a dry spot where one could rest one's tired
bones. And the horses were forced to stand outdoors, freezing. At last we
were able to march back to a small village near Dun on the Maas River.
Hot, summerlike days followed. Every morning we practiced a mock attack on the nearby hills of the Maas River, an attack which was to become real very soon. In the distance there was the loud and penetrating
rumble of the fiery barrage at Verdun. The mood was solemn and despite
the buoyant rhythms of military music one could see only stolid faces.
Everyone was aware of the seriousness of the task ahead of us. Once
again we took part in a solemn field service before marching off to the
front on May 20.

It was late afternoon with the sun beating down relentlessly, as we
arrived in the forest of Sept Sarges near Malancourt and Béthincourt
[Map 11]. We made the last preparations for the attack. Every soldier
received enough provisions for several days, as well as tools of all kinds:
big and small shovels, pickaxes, hand grenades, flame-throwers, barbed
wire, and so forth. Corporals had already been sent ahead to serve as
leaders. They came back, rushed and exhausted, with frightful descriptions of what they had seen. We were able to see some of this from a
nearby mountain top. It certainly was an unforgettable sight. Far in the
distance we observed shells bursting in fire balls. In this witches' cauldron clouds of smoke and earth and rocks were shooting up in huge ghastly
fountains, and the red, green, and white star shells that were rising added
magnificent color to the scene. And then it was dusk and we saw the
gruesome destruction of the villages of Malancourt and Béthincourt;
and the entire region a network of communication and defense trenches.
As far as the eye could see, shells had left the land torn up and furrowed.
We were overwhelmed by a feeling of hopelessness, *Lasciate ogni speranza*
["Abandon all hope" from Dante's "Inferno"]. Here we had to push through,
exposed to a barrage of gunfire that covered miles and miles. When darkness fell we started marching, the ever jolly Lieutenant Trabert by my
side. From the artillery emplacements on our way came the low thunder
of guns. There was a never ending hissing and roaring above us. At last it
had turned completely dark. The companies now marched separately. At
first walking wasn't too difficult on the road and on the unpaved foot-
paths, but then came shell-scarred fields with dead soldiers lying here and

there. A repulsive odor filled the air. We had to watch our steps carefully to avoid nasty falls and, besides, we got constantly entangled in barbed wire and telephone cables lying around on the ground. Then we came through a trench again but only for a short while.

A big, open, low-lying field lay before us. Crater upon crater. Every 100 meters there were relay runners who showed us the way. If it had been tough going up to now, things became worse by the minute. We stumbled from shell-hole to shell-hole with bullets buzzing all around us and shells hitting the ground here and there. At that moment I fell into one of the shell-holes, turning my ankle. I was barely able to walk from the fierce pain it caused, especially since I was straining under the heavy weight of my backpack and other gear. We finally reached a battalion dugout. I asked for directions when one of the officers called out, "You poor devil, you are headed in the wrong direction!" Another soldier showed us the way and we reached the command post of our own battalion at last.

I climbed down into a deep trench where Captain Pfannstiehl and his orderly sat bent over maps. After a short rest we received further orders. Our trenches were only 100 meters away, a distance we finally covered in the darkness, stumbling, lunging ahead. "This is the company commander's dugout," a cheerful voice called out. It was Corporal Garner whom we had sent ahead, one of those who would not get unnerved and was always in a good mood. The so-called dugout was a hole in the ground, covered with a few branches that served as a roof. Thank God we had made it to the front line, and in pretty good shape at that. I threw my things in a corner and squatted next to them, immediately lighting a cigar for comfort. Only then did I take a closer look. In no way could you call this a regular fortified trench. Actually these were barely connected shell-craters, offering no protection whatsoever from artillery fire. That's why my men became quite confused, having been accustomed to neatly constructed trenches. They kept on walking, thinking they would find the trench closer up front. I tried in vain to call them back. A number of them actually did end up in enemy trenches, where they received a friendly welcome by the French. Only one courageous fellow came back. The moment a German shell hit causing confusion among the French, he took off running like mad, back into our trenches without being hit by enemy bullets. This is a true story; it's too bad I forgot the soldier's name.

We now started preparations from our position for the forthcoming attack; the assault troop with their flamethrowers, the machine-gunners, after that the units of our company, and, finally, the soldiers who were to follow, bringing the equipment, ammunition, etc. The attack was to be

The cratered fields near Verdun. Lt. R. states: "Terrain lost recently near Verdun: The Albein-ravine east of the Thiaumont Works with watch outpost of the Thiaumont Forest." The arrow, *left*, below ridge, points to a communication trench, and the "P" in the upper lefthand corner stands for "Pfeffer Ridge," according to Lt. R.

preceded by a two-hour barrage of fire to start at dawn. My company was positioned at the right wing of the attack, which meant we could expect severe machine gun fire from the flank. Our artillery fire started after midnight, a very nerve-wracking ordeal, even for us. I sat in my corner, chewing on my cigar. It felt as though a vibrating, vaulted ceiling was above us, caused by the roar and roll of the approaching shrapnel. Above our heads the heaviest shells came roaring down precipitously, leaving us breathless, and unnerving spirit and mind. We were lost souls lying there, helpless, in our shell-holes. The French trench couldn't be more than 200 meters away at the most, and the hail of shrapnel landed in our trenches. From the start our shots came up too short. In the end our own artillery fire kept zeroing in on us instead of on the enemy so that we had wounded soldiers and were forced to retreat from our trenches. I fired off green star-shells as warning signals for the artillery, but to no avail. Our artillery fire came closer and closer. We finally realized that the artillery attack had hardly made a dent in the French lines and an all-out assault at this time seemed hopeless. So, actually no attack took place. Instead the French had become aware of our location.

The next morning the sun came up and after the turmoil of the past night, revived us a bit with its warmth. We felt completely worn out, and yet the main job still lay ahead. And we were not in the best mood, after our first unsuccessful artillery assault. Besides, we had suffered a number of casualties. We were rather depressed as we sat at the mountainside and looked at the long, stretched-out back of Hill Mort Homme [Dead Man's Hill]. On both sides volleys of shells hitting the ground exploded upwards. Where we were sitting there had once been a healthy forest. Now there were only a few tree stumps staring at the sky. As far as the eye could see was one huge field of craters not unlike a moonscape, where all life seems to have perished.

In the afternoon the barrage of fire was going to be repeated, and we in line with our orders finally carry out our planned attack. This time the artillery fire was right on target, and after approximately one hour it gained hurricane force. We had never experienced anything like it, and we were shaken to the core at this terrible, elemental power of the whistling, roaring shells, which finally exploded in enemy lines just 200 meters in front of us. Never, not even when we were under enemy barrage ourselves, did I become conscious of the wretchedness and insignificance of human existence amid such terrifying forces than at precisely this moment, when man stood utterly defenseless, facing annihilation. I cowered in my corner smoking one cigar after another to stimulate my frayed nerves. I picked up a newspaper from the floor. It was an issue of the "Matin" and I started reading. They spoke triumphantly of the great food shortages in Germany, but I was still paying close attention to what was going on at the enemy's front line. I noticed that there was a constant crackling noise of enemy infantry fire from the right. If the infantry was still able to shoot, while being subjected to our heavy fire, then we could count, without a doubt, on strong resistance and great difficulties during our attack. Ever closer came the big moment when we would have to get out of our trenches, the moment that would answer the question "To be or not to be!"

Now there was only half an hour left, now twenty minutes, now fifteen minutes, now ten minutes. One more time I muster my small troop, we check our watches, and I give last orders for the attack. We tie down our helmets, check on our weapons. We are ready. Lieutenant Trabert waves and shouts, "Time is up!" Two minutes left. One minute. At that moment I see our men on the far left rushing forward. A brief halt, then I see them jump on. In a flash we, too, are out of our dugout running forward across the cratered fields. Machine gun fire awaits us. We manage to advance about

100 meters. Hand grenades fly all around us. We, too, throw hand grenades, but only a few, for one-third of our company is scattered about the terrain, riddled with bullets or shredded to pieces. At last I lie there on the edge of a shell crater alone with a few men. I cannot make out if anyone else of our men is still moving. The French continue to throw hand grenades and shower us with machine gun fire. I duck down with two of my men and we try covering ourselves with our spades. A sharp explosion next to me causes me to look up. A stream of blood is running down my neighbors's temple. Without a sound or shudder he collapses straight in front of me. I, myself, have blood running from under my helmet over my face. For a little while I use the corpse as a cover. Then I grab the body and pull it behind me, gasping, all the while squatting down to avoid being hit by the enemy fire, until he rolls down into the shell-crater. Only his head is above the rim and his broken eyes keep staring at me. I keep digging and throw the earth backward. When I turn around again, I see the body of the dead soldier covered with earth with only his head sticking out. Meantime other soldiers have joined the dead soldier in the crater. What a pitiful sight! There they sit, the poor souls, with squashed arms and legs and eyes shot out. Others with abdominal wounds lie there dying.

And thus evening fell. The shooting gradually died down until we heard only single shots. Only after the sun had disappeared behind the horizon was it safe for me to go to the battalion commander's dugout to receive further orders. I had hardly walked a few steps when I felt a violent pain in my ankle. Disregarding my sprained ankle, I had kept jumping forward during the attack so that now I was unable to pull my boot from my swollen foot. I dragged myself as best I could to an underground dressing station, where the doctor diagnosed a severe sprain and a hemorrhage and sent me to the field hospital. I managed to report to the battalion commander to hand over the command of my company. I knew I wouldn't be able to walk across shell-scarred fields. So for now I lay down on the ground where I was, and after a night without sleep I dozed off. There was no more thought of danger; all I wanted was rest. It was a starlit mild spring night. Airplanes and a dirigible moved along in the sky, seemingly undisturbed and safe, despite volleys of shrapnel. So I lay there for a while not moving, and the horrors of the day slowly subsided in my heart. Then, all of a sudden, someone nudged me with his foot and called out, "*Kamerad*, if you are wounded, get yourself up and out of here." I tried once more to walk back, but turned my ankle even more, fell into a deep crater where I had to stay put, cursing. I heard voices. Two men appeared above the rim shouting, "Are you wounded?" I was delirious with joy when I realized these two men were medics who were taking me to the field hospital.

A few days later I was in Heidelberg where I found rest and recuperation for a while before being sent home on leave. Toward the end of May 1916, the German troops had established an uninterrupted front line from the woods of Malancourt across Hill 304-Mort Homme-Cumières to the Maas River. But then we were deadlocked again. The battles for Verdun continued undecided into July 1916, when the last great German offensive against Fort Souville on July 11, 1916, failed also. With that the drama of Verdun had come to an end.

Chapter Eight

Campaign in East Galicia, 1916–1917

The Brusilov Offensive, 1916 [Map 12]

In June 1916, after initial successes by the Austrians on the Italian front, the Brusilov offensive had taken hold, so that the Austro-Hungarian front line was broken by this enormous, unexpected thrust. The Bukowina region had been lost, and in Wolhymin and Galicia the Russian offensive had only now come to a gradual halt. In the south the offensive had surged to the top of the Carpathian Mountains. Russian troops were threatening to cross into Hungary. In Galicia their assault troops were poised to attack Lemberg, after having advanced almost as far as Zloczow.

In August 1916, I left the Reserve-Battalion, Gera-Reuss, along with several fellow-officers. This time we were headed east. Our destination was east of Lemberg in Galicia. We had decided from the start that we would travel by way of Wien [Vienna] and Budapest. We came through the beautiful Vogtland [area in Central Germany, near the Czech border] until, toward evening, we arrived in Eger in the Breisgau, once the city of Wallenstein "fame." [Eger is today's Cheb in the Czech Republic. General Wallenstein was assassinated here in 1634.] The military seemed to be everywhere. However, we could not stay very long, and the very same evening we were on our way to Vienna. The next day we did as much sightseeing as we could: the Prater [Amusement Park], the Hofburg [residential palace], theaters, and all other places worth seeing in the imperial city, but by noontime the next day, the train was taking us to the Hungarian capital. It was still very summery and we were able to admire at our leisure the magnificent castle and the parliament building of Budapest. There were a lot of people milling about along the piers of the Danube, as well as in the elegant cafés. Men in uniforms dominated the scene. The

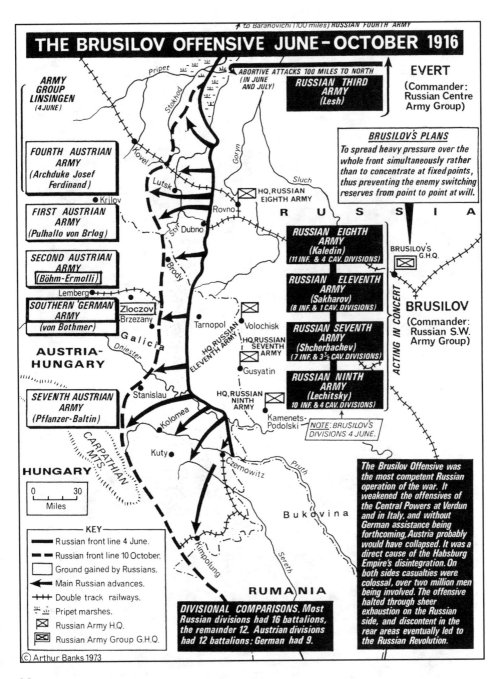

THE BRUSILOV OFFENSIVE JUNE-OCTOBER 1916

to Baranovichi (100 miles) RUSSIAN FOURTH ARMY

ARMY GROUP LINSINGEN (4 JUNE)

ABORTIVE ATTACKS 100 MILES TO NORTH (IN JUNE AND JULY)

RUSSIAN THIRD ARMY (Lesh)

EVERT (Commander: Russian Centre Army Group)

FOURTH AUSTRIAN ARMY (Archduke Josef Ferdinand)

FIRST AUSTRIAN ARMY (Pulhallo von Brlog)

SECOND AUSTRIAN ARMY (Böhm-Ermolli)

SOUTHERN GERMAN ARMY (von Bothmer)

AUSTRIA-HUNGARY

SEVENTH AUSTRIAN ARMY (Pflanzer-Baltin)

HUNGARY

BRUSILOV'S PLANS
To spread heavy pressure over the whole front simultaneously rather than to concentrate at fixed points, thus preventing the enemy switching reserves from point to point at will.

HQ,RUSSIAN EIGHTH ARMY

R U S S I A

RUSSIAN EIGHTH ARMY (Kaledin) (11 INF. & 4 CAV. DIVISIONS)

BRUSILOV'S G.H.Q.

RUSSIAN ELEVENTH ARMY (Sakharov) (8 INF. & 1 CAV. DIVISIONS)

BRUSILOV (Commander: Russian S.W. Army Group)

ACTING IN CONCERT

RUSSIAN SEVENTH ARMY (Shcherbachev) (7 INF. & 3½ CAV. DIVISIONS)

RUSSIAN NINTH ARMY (Lechitsky) (10 INF. & 4 CAV. DIVISIONS)

HQ,RUSSIAN ELEVENTH ARMY

HQ,RUSSIAN SEVENTH ARMY

HQ,RUSSIAN NINTH ARMY

NOTE: BRUSILOV'S DIVISIONS 4 JUNE.

Krilov · Lutsk · Rovno · Dubno · Brody · Lemberg · Zloczov · Brzezany · Tarnopol · Volochisk · Gusyatin · Stanislau · Kolomea · Kuty · Czernowitz · Kamenets-Podolski

Pripet · Stokhod · Kovel · Styr · Goryn · Sluch · Galicia · Dniester · CARPATHIAN MTS.

B u k o v i n a

Pruth · Sereth · Kimpolung

RUMANIA

The Brusilov Offensive was the most competent Russian operation of the war. It weakened the offensives of the Central Powers at Verdun and in Italy, and without German assistance being forthcoming, Austria probably would have collapsed. It was a direct cause of the Habsburg Empire's disintegration. On both sides casualties were colossal, over two million men being involved. The offensive halted through sheer exhaustion on the Russian side, and discontent in the rear areas eventually led to the Russian Revolution.

DIVISIONAL COMPARISONS. Most Russian divisions had 16 battalions, the remainder 12. Austrian divisions had 12 battalions; German had 9.

0   30
Miles

KEY
— Russian front line 4 June.
■ ■ ■ Russian front line 10 October.
☐ Ground gained by Russians.
◀— Main Russian advances.
+++ Double track railways.
Pripet marshes.
⊠ Russian Army H.Q.
⊠ Russian Army Group G.H.Q.

© Arthur Banks 1973

Map 12

The Brusilov Offensive: June-October 1916

In August 1916 Lt. R. and fellow officers arrived in Lemberg to return to the front in the hilly terrain of Zloczov.

A field postcard.

The printed message reads: "East Galicia, German field kitchen before departure to the front line." Added, in author's handwriting: "12th L. 32." (L = Landwehr) These names are listed on the back: "Right, Sergeant Bergen; Private Zierentz; Private Koch...Driver ("coachman") Hesbig."

"At the Field Kitchen"

The fellow, *far left, seated*, is smoking a pipe. *Center, right*, two men are enjoying a hot meal. The three boys, in front, seem to have joined the group.

theaters were open for the season and tuneful melodies echoed from dance pavilions and cafés. Nevertheless, the public mood was depressed, and for good reasons.

On the Move Again

Lemberg was our destination [Map 12]. The train trip took all night. In the evening the walls of the Carpathian Mountains were towering above us and when we peeked through the fogged-up windows, we could see that we were already traveling through the plains of Galicia and approaching Lemberg. The large railroad station was partially destroyed. A streetcar took us through the less than beautiful suburbs, with their somewhat Slavic character, into the inner city which seemed quite modern with its beautiful boulevards and imposing buildings. The Jewish population dominated the streets. We couldn't stay very long since we had already made telephone contact with our division and received orders to proceed to the division staff-quarters in Kazimirowka. Soon we were sitting in a train that was once again eastward bound. But such comfortable transportation would end soon. We had learned through experience how trying the last miles to the front could be on the railroad. Towards the end the train slows down to a crawl, with us in a cattle car, until finally they simply drop us somewhere, in an open field with no shelter in sight, often at night in cold and rainy weather.

Slowly the train moved through the plains of Galicia. Marshes and meadows alternated with fertile fields of grain. Soon we left the pastures with their cattle behind us and entered the hilly terrain of Zloczow. We had a longer stop-over there. The town was crowded with German troops. An endless stream of wagons was moving toward the front, whipping up white dust clouds from the road. The din of cannons thundering and star-shells rising in the distance were a reminder that the front line was very near. We moved through the mountainous canyons of Zarwanika toward our destination, the town of Kazimirowka. The division had sent a *Panje* wagon to pick us up and take us to the village.

Upon my arrival at the division's staff quarters I was overjoyed to find our former regiment-adjutant from Regiment No. 96, Captain Heldberg, now the 2nd adjutant of the 197th Infantry Division. My company and I were assigned to this very unit. The staff quarters in primitive peasant huts were very plain and modest. After having been presented to our Division Commander, His Excellency Wilhelmi, we drove on to our regiment's staff where I was assigned company commander to the 12th Company of the Landwehr Infantry Regiment No. 32.

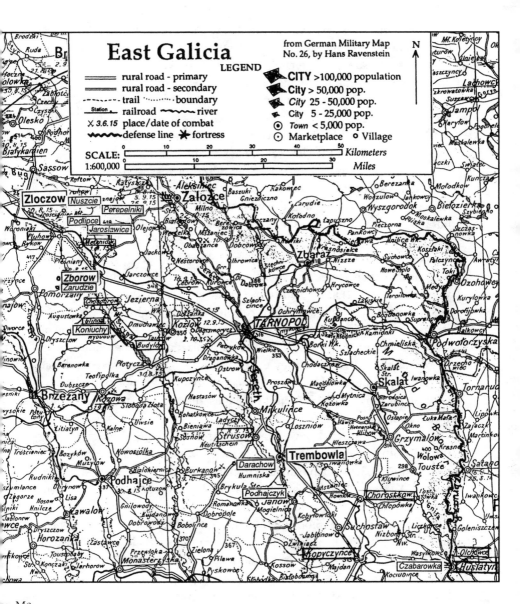

ıp M2

German Military Map, East Galicia

part of the 197th Infantry Division, Lt. R. and his Regiment No. 32 took part in a counteroffensive
itheast of Zloczow (Zloczov) in 1916 and again in 1917. The latter campaign ended near Husiatyn (lower
ht hand corner). The dates shown are those of earlier battles in 1915.

So there we were, back at the front where, together with our new fellow officers, we were to experience much sadness, but also joy. It was a gorgeous late summer afternoon when nature was still in full splendor, and in the fields the heavy stalks of grain were swaying back and forth. In the shady orchard we were introduced to more fellow officers, among them the young Lieutenant Ewald, whom we called "dolly," and Lieutenant Nestler, as well as the always cheerful Sergeant Mittelstädt from the machine gun company, who was always ready to crack a joke.

The front line was only a few hundred meters in front of us. Still, everything seemed very peaceful. There was hardly any shooting. Only a few large shell craters along the way were proof that here such peace was not always the order of the day. The traditional mobile open-field battles had only recently come to a standstill, then turning into fixed positional warfare. At the bottom of a protected hillside, the troops were digging trenches for themselves and their horses. Everything around here was as yet unfinished so that we had to use every minute for the construction of fortifications and communication trenches to the front line. In the evening it was far less quiet in the trenches. At night, when we were asleep on our straw sacks in a *Panje* hut, rifle bullets whizzed past the windows and there was the danger that they would crash through the weak mud walls of our little house. The feeling of safety that we knew from home was once again gone. This was quite obvious the very first evening, and it would soon get worse.

Early the next day we started marching along the Strypa Bogs through often marshy areas to Jaroslawice, where we joined our companies. It was the day when Rumania declared war on Germany [August 27, 1916]. We could therefore assume that the Russians here in Galicia would soon continue their offensive that had been so successful until now. My company sergeant, a short man by the name of Bergen, who in peace times was a tailor in Bürgel in Thuringia, hence nicknamed Sergeant "Zwirn" [thread], accompanied me to our trench installation approximately 300 meters away from his quarters. Everything was still unfinished. There was no safe communication trench leading to the front so that one had to run across the open field. Up to now this was not yet too dangerous since the Russian trenches were still pretty far away. Our trenches were deep and laid out in a regular pattern. However, dugouts and other covers against artillery fire were only now being built. The first thing I did was to survey the area and the position of our trenches. Before us was a small village, and the Russians were positioned across from us on medium range hills. In broad daylight we could clearly see individual Russians moving about. The mountain ridge of the Zlota Gora [Gold Mountain] rose far to the right, where we could observe little shrapnel clouds flying in the air. Behind us in the valley we saw the village of Jaroslawice with its beautiful park and palatial manor still looking quite imposing. The chimney of the distillery rose above the low terrain. That's where the field hospital was located.

Digging In

Down there along a slope they were digging trenches for the reserves. Carpenters and a ground crew were working hard around the clock. They cut down trees and used them to make everything they needed for the trenches. Across the empty field they were dragging boards, stakes, poles, wire, and beams to the trenches. It was still possible to work in relative peace, for the artillery sent its volleys only infrequently. Expecting the Russian assault any time, we wanted to be well fortified in our trenches as quickly as possible. In the beginning there was nothing that might have protected us against shrapnel and shells. As for myself, I camped outdoors at first. My orderly and I had arranged ourselves in a communication trench where I made myself comfortable on the ground. For the night we made a roof from a tarp to protect us from the cool air in the morning. That worked pretty well at first. But as the weather got colder, and the Russian artillery began systematically to get a range of our trenches, we dug a large hole into a trench wall and propped it up with boards and beams. Of course, it was barely high enough for us to sit in. On beautiful, sunny days we sat happily outdoors most of the time, seeking cover in our dugout only when there was artillery fire or at night. Eventually we managed at least to increase the depth of our trench by a few steps, which protected us somewhat.

And so the month of August passed with us working steadily and very, very hard. Each one of us tried to outdo the other in his effort to provide us with a safe shelter as soon as possible. Every day I carefully observed the Russian positions and made maps and sketches. Daily, the Russians dug new trenches on their side. I had to carefully pinpoint their position with my field glasses in order to recognize anything, for the Russians had covered their new trenches meticulously with sheaves of grain. They had already descended the slope on their side and were now extending their trenches up our hillside. Consequently, combat activities from our side were increased. Every night our patrols went out to reconnoiter the enemy's position and their nocturnal activities. This often developed into heavier shoot-outs resulting, unfortunately, in a number of soldiers killed or wounded. During these nights that were anything but

October 10, 1916, in Galicia, Russia: "You see here the entrance to my dugout near the village of Jaroslawice. This is still my 'home.' Lt. Rosenhainer." Notice the two cottages to the left with sod-covered roofs.

quiet we didn't get much sleep. Besides that, we had to strengthen the wire barricades in front of our trenches or even put up new ones. And that wasn't easy during those moonlit nights when the Russians were able to observe exactly what was going on. Meanwhile, the construction of my command post dugout had proceeded quite well. As many as ten steps now led down into the ground, and to the right enough space had been created in the dugout to house myself, my orderlies, and the telephone operators. The Russians were now stepping up their firing activity more and more. Their trenches and ours were by now only 250 meters apart. There was nothing we could do about it. Even though we were bombarding them with shrapnel, mines, and rifle fire, the next morning they had new trenches in place.

Battles near Jaroslavice, September 1916

More serious battles were looming ahead that were to last from August 31 to September 9, 1916. Even before that there had been strong combat activity from both sides. At the Zlota Gora, especially, fighting increased steadily. More and more frequently we saw black pillars rising to the sky and heard the muffled sound of shells crashing down over there. Soon the entire mountain was enveloped by clouds of smoke and dust. From our trench we had a perfect view of the entire area. Everybody's eyes were fixed on the ridge of the Zlota Gora because what was unraveling before our eyes there might very well determine our fate, too. If the Russians managed to break through, we, too, would be lost. What we saw was indeed an exciting spectacle. Suddenly, out of the smoke and dust we noticed long open lines of soldiers emerging, alternately stopping and running back across the fields. They quickly reached the woods of Meteniow [Map M2]. In short order I received a phone call from our battalion-commander (Captain Scheer), "Our situation has taken on a turn for the worse: The Russians have broken through the lines at Zlota Gora." And he was right! We saw new lines of skirmishers. To be sure, these were Russians. They pushed forward into our artillery positions and came already dangerously close behind our backs. But at this point they encountered strong resistance. Our desperate gunners were defending themselves with hand grenades and carbines, and when the Jägerbatallion [German riflemen], who had just now arrived from home, stormed the Russians, they had to retreat. They were thrown back almost to their starting point. Later we took back even the last of our lost trenches. Heavy fighting took place also south of us near Perepelniki [Map M2] where the Russians initially had some success, but they could not sustain it for long.

There followed a few quiet days—beautiful, sunny September days. Getting up early in the morning from our straw "beds," with the sun shining brightly above, we no longer thought of war. The farmers were harvesting their crops in the fields while the cattle were grazing in the pastures below. Everywhere you looked you could see ripening fruit and vegetables and soon the first potatoes would be harvested. Our field kitchen had it a lot easier now, for everything that grew in our range of fire was ours. The long duration of the war contributed to our feeling that the trenches were almost second home, and we gave their improvements much thought and tender, loving care. We were always trying to think of new means and ways to make life in our trenches more pleasant and more comfortable. However, right now we had to place more emphasis on developing trenches with strong defense capabilities, for the Russians wouldn't leave us alone. How often was I chased out of my little chamber in the trench by bursting shrapnel! It was calmest in the early morning hours.

On September 16, 1916, I had gotten up very early. It was a fine, sunny autumn morning. Nothing stirred as I walked quietly through the trench in order to check up on the enemy positions. Suddenly a roar in the air and a black fountain of smoke and dust shot upwards. Instantly the peaceful calm of this morning hour was shattered. I hurried to my dug-out to continue my observations. More and more heavy explosions fol-lowed. We soon were quite sure that we could expect a Russian attack shortly. Everybody rushed into their protective shelter; only a few ob-servers remained at their posts. The fiery barrage directed toward our trenches grew stronger and stronger. Then, finally, our artillery started shooting, sending heavy shrapnel into enemy lines, wreaking havoc. Our defensive fire became so effective that the Russians hardly dared leave their trenches, and the day ended without giving them the hoped-for vic-tory. The barrage didn't end until late afternoon, and when we came out of our trenches again into broad daylight we found that our work was just beginning. The wounded had to be bandaged and taken away. The damaged trenches had to be repaired as best we could, so they would be able to withstand another onslaught. Out front we worked to repair the damaged wire barricades. Ammunition and provisions were replenished because we had to count on the fighting to pick up again soon. And so we lay down on our make-shift beds, tired and weary, worrying about what would happen next.

However, the next morning started out very peaceful and quiet. I was therefore able to set out for the company next to us to survey the Russian positions from there. I had with me a stereo-telescope, and along with an artillery lieutenant (Lieutenant Ostermann, Rgt. 261) I walked to a forward sap trench for a better view [narrow trench made by digging at an angle from an existing trench]. We had hardly set up our telescope when there was a deafening explosion right next to us. A shell had hit, showering us with a hail of rocks and debris. In a flash we were back in the trench with our big telescope. A while later, the company commander of the neighboring company (Infantry Regiment 273) and I were seated comfortably in his dugout with a cup of coffee. Still, a strange, restless feeling made me leave soon and I returned to my company's quarters. Already, strong enemy fire had begun in the direction of our trenches. Was I glad to be out of harm's way when I was back in my dugout!

Outside, the barrage grew stronger and stronger. Without delay, the guards at the outposts sent alarming news: They had already had a number of men dead or wounded. Their own guard posts had become indefensible in the heavy artillery fire so that they had to withdraw to our combat trenches. The battalion command phoned to find out what the situation was. I was still able to answer. But soon the wires were shot down and, risking their lives, the telephone operators tried hard to repair them. Yet, in the end, all communication was cut off. And so my brave messenger, Corporal Hennlein, ran through volleys of exploding shells and smoking gun powder to deliver important messages. I often went to the exit to observe what was going on: There was a terrifying howling and whining in the air. Heavy shells hit our trench walls with a roar. Shell fragments and shrapnel were ripping through the air. I went back inside. And now one shell after another came crashing down on our dugout with terrifying force, violently shaking the entire structure of our entrenchment. The top soil had already been swept away. Inside we kept hearing cracking and banging noises. The walls had only weak supports and one side wall was about to cave in. One direct hit on the trench entrance would have sufficed to bury us all. A lot of wounded had taken refuge here and were now sitting deep down inside the trench. We could hear their moaning and groaning.

Soon I couldn't stand it much longer inside the trench. I just had to see for myself; above all, I wanted to know just when the Russian infantry attack would begin. More dead than alive, I arrived at the left wing of my company from where I had a fair view across the terrain. The terrible fire continued unabated. The entire trench was enveloped by a single vibrating cloud of exploding shrapnel. But high in the air our heavy German fire was headed over to the Russians with a roar. That was comforting music to our ears. The parapets had been severely hit and our old dugouts had collapsed in the trenches. I groped my way over deformed bodies, and then I had to frantically squeeze into a corner to let a volley of shrapnel pass. The wounded were calling for help; stretcher-bearers hurried past. My orderly and I were swept off our feet and landed in a corner just as we arrived at the combat trench of our left wing. Shells had exploded nearby and the air pressure had simply blown us away. We wanted to peek over the parapet when machine guns started roaring and explosives came flying like thousands of sharp knives all too closely above our heads. The Russians had left their trenches, ready to attack us with their hand grenades, that much we knew. So far they were still hiding from our view in lower terrain. At that moment a tremendously loud roar rose up above our heads: German shells of every caliber were howling and bellowing over to the Russians. We raised our heads and drew a sigh of relief. But the right wing of my company was badly hit. The word was that the enemy had broken through the line. I therefore hurried to the right at once.

As I was looking across the parapet I saw on the right how our men were rushing with their bayonets forward across the empty field. The Russians had penetrated the neighboring 11th Company and had gotten as far as the cemetery and the battalion staff headquarters. At that moment the reserve machine gunners under Lieutenant Ewald started shooting and they drove the enemy back. The enemy had penetrated the right wing of my company as well, but Lieutenant Hentzenröder with his brave unit had immediately thrown them out again. We began fighting the enemy man to man. The dead were lying in and around the trenches staring at us blindly. But we stood our ground, and by nightfall, all became quiet around us and in us. Exhausted from all the exertion and turmoil, I staggered back into my dugout.

That day we had incurred huge losses of dead and wounded, and the next day in the village of Jaroslawice they were placed in a long row to be buried in a mass grave. The village and, above all, the manor, had suffered greatly from the artillery fire. Some of the strong, magnificent trees of the park were broken like matches.

We were not to remain in these trenches much longer. As early as next morning we pulled out for a period of rest in Jaroslawice. It was pitch dark when we started and one of those rare mild autumn nights. Very quietly we left Kazimirowka. Both palace and park were silhouetted pale and phantomlike against the night sky. Infantry bullets whizzed eerily about our ears as we walked across the little bridge. Bullets were hitting trees, others ricocheted off rocks. We were somewhat unnerved; still the troops moved forward calmly and steadily. No one could change his fate; after all, that was entirely left to chance. Tired and fatigued from lack of sleep, we arrived in Kazimirowka to get a few hours sleep on beds of straw (September 21, '16). Were we ever relieved to be able to walk around freely for a while!

September 23 was another beautiful sunny autumn day. I took advantage of the local baths. After that I went for a little walk with First Lieutenant Kallenbach, my old friend from our school days in Eisenach [city in Thuringia.] We came to a hilltop from where we had a good view of the entrenchments. There had been renewed activity along the front. I didn't think much of it at first. But Kallenbach felt that this shooting was unusually strong, probably a sign that another attack was in the making. However, we didn't let that bother us, and strolled back to the village. Right away an orderly came toward us with the order that the battalion had just been placed on alert and that Lieutenant Rosenhainer was to report at once to the battalion commander, Captain Scheer. I got ready immediately and reported to the battalion's staff. I was to ride to the front immediately, after obtaining further orders from the division commander in Wolzkowce. My company was to start marching and follow me at once. Within minutes I had mounted my horse and was on my way to Wolzkowce.

At the front, enemy artillery fire was coming down steadily on our trenches, and I saw huge columns of smoke rise up. My horse was getting restless, and when we passed a German howitzer battery that just then started firing, causing the shells to zoom above our heads with a loud howling sound, my horse started spinning around. I couldn't hold it in check and had to dismount and turn it over to a gunner who led it into a stable. When I arrived at the division on foot, the general himself gave me my orders. For now I was to stay in the village with my company as a reserve unit and, when needed, to move into the frontal trenches. Soon my company arrived, and we started digging trenches in order to be protected against possible artillery attacks. Then the steaming field kitchen arrived and we were given something to eat. Standing there we had hardly taken a few bites when the first heavy shell crashed into the village. We were ordered to march at once. We dropped our food into the grass and off we went.

We had to march on without any cover for about two and one half kilometers through a very long valley, where we could easily be seen by the enemy. Right off we were confronted again by heavy shells near the outskirts of the village. We jumped forward, always two at a time, at 50 meter intervals. I was running in front with my orderly. The trail we followed was along a slope, on the left side. With a thunderous noise the explosives kept rolling across the valley. They plunged like wild monsters into the swampy terrain, sending mud, water, and clumps of grass flying into the air. Our company moved forward in a long single file. Everywhere you could see small clouds of shrapnel; the entire valley had come to life. We began a mad run for our lives: At times we slowed down, but during renewed firing, picked up speed again to reach a low area for cover. Then again we stayed glued to the ground until a shooting barrage subsided. At last, gasping for breath, and utterly exhausted, I reached an artillery position. Here I could catch my breath and wait for my company to catch up. The gunners in their relatively safe dugouts were quite chipper and treated me to beverages and cigars. They felt that a Russian attack was imminent. Then we were off again. On the other side of the valley some of my men were still running through the shrapnel fire, but they tried to avoid it by turning to the right. Thank God, most of them made it safely. We were soon protected by a mountain, and when we arrived at the regiment's command post, we were safe.

I called my company together and we proceeded to a gravel-pit, our destination. Up front the drumfire continued. We were right behind the front line. This was no time to sit around and wait. We had to dig quickly in to be protected from possible artillery fire. What a commotion and what a mess in all this dirt and sand! Directly behind us were German batteries, shooting like mad. A crash and a bang: Dirt, rocks, and metal were flying around our heads. The wounded were screaming and crying for help. One Russian artillery shell had exploded in our sand-pit. The Russians had detected us in our hide-away. We immediately took full cover until it finally got dark and things calmed down. Our stomachs were growling for at the moment the field kitchens had, of course, no way of getting to us, and earlier we had had to throw away our noon meal.

That very same evening I was ordered to set out with my company to support and help the 2nd Battalion which had suffered extremely heavy losses. At dusk we left our sand-pit without making a sound and marched through the valley for about three quarters of an hour. Things had quieted down somewhat and the artillery was silent. Star-shells, in larger numbers than usual, were lighting up the area in front of the trenches. Up front, shots were hammering away and shells were flying around us just as if in the butts on a firing range. The Second Battalion had suffered heavy losses. The less seriously wounded were still coming from the front and the serious casualties were taken away. The enemy fire had done extensive damage: The trenches were shot to pieces and the wire barricades were strewn about, fragmented. This is where my men came in and they worked almost all through the night. For one, the trench walkways had to be restored. Debris, boards, and beams had to be removed. Temporary wire mazes had to be hauled to the site from miles away, to replace the damaged ones. In the constant infantry fire, these were death-defying tasks. I went to see my company commander (Lieutenant Häuser). His dugout had remained intact. I was glad to get something to eat and drink. Nearby was a dugout that had completely collapsed and two officers were buried underneath. One soldier walked by whose whole body was shaking; he was suffering from shell-shock. By early dawn, the trench was once again operative and ready for defense. We had accomplished our mission and could now return to our sand-pit, hoping for a few hours' rest and some sleep.

The sky was overcast and soon it started raining cats and dogs. There probably wouldn't be any more Russian attacks for now, but there we were sitting in this sand-pit, exposed to the weather. It didn't take long for the water to seep through the thin roofs that we had made temporarily with tarps. Our individual sand-pits turned into puddles. There was nothing we could do. Soon we were completely drenched. This miserable existence lasted fully three days. On the third day we simply couldn't stand it any longer and left to settle in a few houses in the village of Jaroslawice [Map M2]. We rerouted telephone cables to remain connected. Now we were at least able to dry our clothes. The field kitchen finally reached us also, even brought us some mail, so that for now we were alright again. Finally the sun managed to break through the clouds again. It was a wonderful morning in the middle of gardens with ripening fruit. We didn't hear any shooting nor the din of battle. Around us was nature in all its freshness and beauty, after an invigorating rain. We went outside to finally dry our clothes completely. At that moment I was called to the phone. I was to report immediately to Battalion Commander Captain Scheer in Wolzkowce to inspect with him some entrenchments that we were to occupy soon. I was quick to get going without my usual morning coffee, accompanied by my orderly, Albin Waider.

We walked along the Jaroslawice path we knew so well, passing the palace gardens in the outskirts of the village, then up the hills from where we had a commanding view of the German and Russian positions, then past artillery posts that were surrounded by shell-craters, then down past the mill in the idyllic valley and into the heavily damaged village of Wolzkowce. Nevertheless, enough buildings were left standing to house staff members and supplies. But their stay here was far from undisturbed and secure because now and then heavy shells hit the village. During our march we had already noticed increasing activity at the front. By now it had accelerated to quite an intensive artillery combat. Even our path to Wolzkowce was not safe. This was not a good omen. At staff headquarters I was received with these words, "What on earth are you doing here? The Russians are attacking and you go for walks in this terrain." So it was true: A Russian attack was imminent. I quickly gulped down a cup of coffee before returning to my company. We took the same route. We had hardly left the village behind when several artillery officers were already coming toward us shouting, "You can't make it across the hills, the perimeter of Jaroslawice is under heavy artillery fire!" We decided to take this route anyway. The further we got, the closer we heard the roar of the guns.

Along our entire route veritable fountains of shell explosions spouted into the air. We ducked down and walked along the ditch alongside the road. Since the entrance to the village was black with clouds of smoke, we quickly turned into a small valley, thinking we would be safe here. But here, too, shrapnel was flying about. Finally we reached our cottage but we didn't stay long because an unexploded shell crashed down very close by, telling us to leave the place as soon as possible. We therefore re-strung the telephone wires on a steep protected slope nearby and dug holes as

The Winter of 1916/17 in the Frozen Trenches of the Mogila Hills near Zarudzie

On the lookout with binoculars.

Company commander Lt. R., to the left. A machine gunner is sitting on the step of the trenches. Several men are equipped with goggles (on caps).

You see here a wattle and daub construction used extensively for trench retaining walls.

Lt. R. with ranging binoculars.

Photo A

Photo A). Sign at the top reads: "Company commander's dugout." Below: "Entrance to my dugout. Position Zarudzie." Signed O. Oettel, Jan. 22, 1917.

Photo B). Caption at the top reads: "My dugout at our position near Zarudzie." Sign behind entrance: "Company dugout 136." Signed O. Oettel, in the field, Jan. 22, 1917.

Photo B

Although my father had placed this photo opposite his descriptions of the battles fought near Lodz, in November 1914, these crosses from 1916 indicate a different time and place (probably east of Lemberg). Cross to the left reads: "Ers. Res. Fritz Kraft fell [in battle], Nov. 16, 1916. Ldw. I.R. 32, #6, 12th Comp." (Lt. R. had been assigned as company commander to this very unit in August 1916.) Cross to the right reads: "Here rests, under God, 2nd Lieutenant Bruno Gretscher, 9th Comp., 4th I.R. 32. Fell [in battle], Nov. 23, 1916."

March 9, 1917. Korzeylow with part of the Mogila Hills.

Early spring brought its own problems with floods and swampy terrain. Zarudzie in the background. Author's comments on the back of photo: "Flood waters near Zarudzie, East Galicia, 3-15-17."

Village of Zarudzie [Map M2], winter 1916/17. Church in the background. *Left*, House No. 63, possibly affixed by German troops. Officer, *on horseback*, meeting up with soldiers and horsedrawn wagon.

best we could for our own protection. In the meantime, the battle in front was in full swing. We were right in the midst of the artillery duel. From our position as a reserve unit we could look over the flank and see the village of Jaroslawice with its manor and the distillery. Shells that crashed down there caused black pillars of smoke to rise to the sky. The manor collapsed, the brick walls of the distillery came tumbling down, trees were split apart, thatched roofs flew through the air, planks and rocks whirled about like so many toys. And then, with a loud boom, the tall chimney of the distillery came crashing down. During all this turmoil we sat there as reserves, awaiting the command to move to the front and lend our support to the fighting units.

The Russians are expanding the perimeter of their firing range more and more. Already shrapnel is whistling above our heads hitting the side of the mountain. Only a few hundred meters away from us small shrapnel clouds are dancing all along the Strypa valley. A terrible bang! Fifty meters in front of us one of the heavy shells hits the soggy ground. The earth trembles and clumps of grass, muddy peat moss and dirt shoot up all around us. It hasn't been too bad, though, the soft ground has simply swallowed up the grenade, and thus muted the force of the explosion. There is a humming noise above us; an airplane appears, dropping several bombs on us but they miss their mark. Still, that airplane makes us a little jittery. The entire area is now filled with one enormous vibrating roar. Then suddenly all is quiet. The tension rises with every passing moment. Will the enemy penetrate the lines? Will we, too, have to fight man to man? Loud riflefire comes from the left. The Russians are attacking. But their attack is halted by our machine gun and infantry fire.

The day ended in our favor, with us not having to defend the front line. For a few days we moved again into another somewhat primitive entrenchment, before settling in for the winter in the trenches of the Mogila Hills near Zarudzie [Map M2].

Winter in the Mogila Hills near Zarudzie

On October 11, 1916, I was sent to the Austrian regiment's staff in Zarudzie by Captain Scheer to discuss my taking over the new positions in the Mogila Hills. I was a lone rider headed into unknown territory. It was already dusk when I approached the village of Uslow. The last rays of the sun left a golden glow on the forlorn crosses of soldiers' graves. Many a mother's son lay buried here in foreign soil. The villages nearby looked friendly, hidden among trees whose yellowing leaves were slowly falling to the ground, a symbol of our own mortality. It had become pitchdark by the time I reached Uslow. My horse stumbled on the rough dirt roads. Now and then I got out my flashight. On entering the village, I was stopped by a Bosnian soldier of the Bosnic-Herzegovinian regiment but he let me pass when he realized I was a German officer. After many hours I finally reached Zarudzie. Only a few small lights glimmered in homes that were scattered over a wide area. Otherwise everything seemed deserted. Suddenly I noticed something moving. "Is this the location of the Bosnian regiment's staff quarters?" I asked a soldier. "No understand German" was the reply. What was I to do? After a long search I finally found an Austrian officer who pointed me in the direction of another village. I finally got to the regiment's staff, after searching for hours in total darkness and after several awkward conversations with Bosnian guards. After having reported to the regiment's commander I was formally invited for dinner. We gathered in a pretty, rustic room and soon enjoyed a hearty meal and a glass of excellent Pilsen beer, for us Germans a treat we hadn't enjoyed in a long time. All the officers were part of the regiment's staff: At the head of the table, the very congenial commander, the Catholic and Islamic chaplains, the short Jewish medical

Lt. R. wrote on the reverse side of photo: "Troop review L.I.R. 32. Front row, left, Boehm-Ermolli; rear, right, Lt. Butz, Adj. II/32, 92 I.R."

officer, the portly adjutant. We talked about our experiences in the war before I finally went to bed in a small farmhouse, dead tired.

On October 11, the battalion left for Zarudzie, and on October 13, we (the 11th and 12th Company) relieved the 1st Bosnic-Herzegovinian Regiment. We now served under the command of the 64th Austrian Infantry Brigade that was part of the Army Böhm-Ermolli. Winter was approaching, and for many months we remained stationed in the frozen trenches by the Mogila Hills. For weeks on end the entrenchments were buried in deepest snow. It was therefore hardly possible to engage in warfare. We rarely heard a shot. This weather was only good for attacks on isolated outposts. Unfortunately, one time the Russians succeeded in doing just that by seizing one of ours. A snowstorm prevented our sentries from watching the enemy, while it helped the Russians, during their assault on a sap trench, to take several of our men prisoner. And then the snow started to melt. The trenches turned into rivulets and the dugouts filled with water. We could only walk around in high boots, and from the Mogila Hills, streams of water came pouring down into our trenches. Their force was so strong they could have powered entire mills. Only by digging more trenches that were sloping downward were we able to remedy the situation. It wasn't easy to dig into the still frozen soil. However, we managed to overcome this deluge.

Gradually spring arrived. The water evaporated and the roads were back to normal. The warm sun revived the vegetation, and the green valleys offered a friendlier sight. Soon our stay in the Mogila Hills came to an end. In April our battalion was pulled out, and we marched almost the entire day to a camp in the woods called "Mogilka." In the middle of a forest they had built very nice wooden barracks. Here we were quartered, supposedly for a rest. But not so you'd notice: Our time was fully taken up with activities, such as building defenses behind the front lines and with drill exercises.

Finally spring arrived in all its splendor. Everything was getting green and blossomed beautifully in the forest. Several times a week in the evening when it was getting dark we'd move out to work on the entrenchments. It took us one to two hours to get there. Those were lovely spring evenings and nights and were treasured by those of us who loved nature and nature's beauty. Only a few kilometers separated us from the front lines, and when the nights were not dark enough we made sure we were covered by marching in low-lying terrain and behind ridges. Most of our work was done near Wolzkowce and Jaroslawice, villages that we were acquainted with from our earlier battles. The trench lines had been staked out during the day and at night we would do the excavating. Breaking up the often extremely hard soil was hard, demanding work. By the time morning dawned we could hardly keep our eyes open and were barely able to move our arms. Sometimes, combat activities flared up on the front line. A long string of star-shells would rise to the sky. There was then the hollow roar of artillery fire and bright flashes of lightning where shells hit the ground.

When morning dawned, we always got ready to leave. We often had to hurry to get out of the danger zone while it was still dark. Up in the sky it was completely light by now, but darkness still covered the ground. Thus protected, we hurried to our camp. Steaming coffee was already waiting for us. We then closed the shutters, and before long we were sound asleep on our make-shift beds.

We had settled in here for a longer stay. For instance, to upgrade our surroundings we created a beautiful garden and flower beds and did all sorts of things to beautify the environment of our camp. We opened up a social center for our troops, and the company's vocal group entertained us many an evening. We didn't work too hard on our company drills. Now and then we drilled in larger units together with Austrian troops, and once the Austrian General Eduard von Böhm-Ermolli reviewed our formation. We now were part of the army unit under von Eben.

The early summer was very dry. The sun beat down relentlessly on parched fields. Grass and grain were stunted in their growth. In addition to worrying about the war we now had to worry about food. The murderous hunger blockade was taking its toll: Even our bread rations were cut. [The reference is to the severe and long blockade of Germany by English ships.] Still, the first days of spring were wonderful. For miles on end our camp was surrounded by vast forests. During our time off I went on long horseback rides in the surrounding area accompanied by my friend, the cheerful staff physician, Dr. Trier from Cologne, and Lieutenant Peters. What a wealth of natural beauty all around us! How uplifting to leave the monotony of a soldier's life behind! What plans we then made for the future and what high hopes we still had for a victorious end of this world war! We then rode to the heights near Zloczow and across to the mountains near the Sereth River. Deep down below us the meandering river, but on the other side dark, silent, and seemingly endless forests. Straw-thatched hamlets looked pretty on the slopes that were covered over many miles by trenches and wire barricades.

In a deeply ridged canyon with forests and streams, our medical officer had created a bath-house, the "Diana-Bath." There one could have tub baths and showers, and outdoors there was even a small swimming pool.

Chapter Nine

Battle in East Galicia, 1917

The Kerenski Offensive, July 1917 [Maps 13a and M2]

Week after week passed and the end of June was approaching. Once again the activities in the theaters of war had reached a high pitch. Even Kerenski's massive troops pulled themselves together once again. Activities intensified along the railroad line Zloczow-Tarnopol. Explosions caused by all calibers of guns were proof that the Russians had readied large numbers of artillery for an attack. Towards the end of June the battle exploded along the entire long line of entrenchments from the Mogila Hills to Zlota Gora and on to Perepelniki. The artillery fire even ended up in our forest camp. My 12th Company was still sleeping in their barracks when two heavy shells crashed very close to the barracks, wiping out our pretty gardens. We could have been in real trouble. There was heavy fighting near Perepelniki, but the Russians were beaten back repeatedly.

Together with our medical officer and Lieutenant Peters, I often went to an elevated observation post in the forest. From there we watched with our binoculars what was happening on the battlefield. In the distance we saw shrapnel exploding and tall pillars of smoke going up on the horizon. Near the Zlota Gora, the old volcano, the scene was one of lightning flashes and thunderous crashing noises.

Supporting our Allies, the Austro-Hungarian Troops

We remained stoic, never dreaming we might have to march again so soon. Then, on the evening of July 1, 1917, quite unexpectedly, "Attention to orders. Assemble at once at the gates of the Mogilka Camp." We rushed into our barracks helter-skelter and hurriedly got our things together. Many

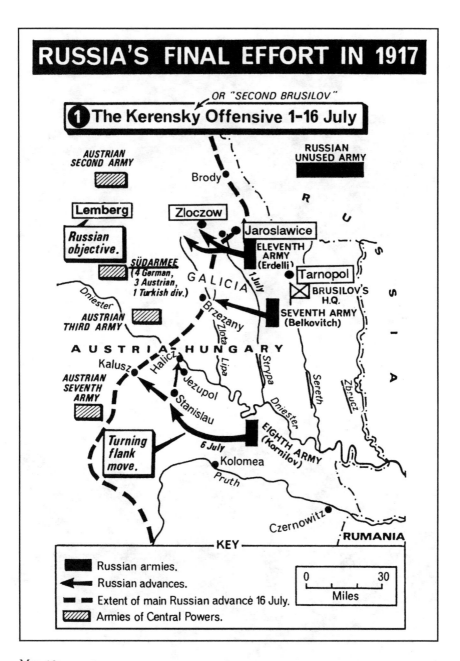

RUSSIA'S FINAL EFFORT IN 1917

OR "SECOND BRUSILOV"

1 The Kerensky Offensive 1-16 July

AUSTRIAN SECOND ARMY

RUSSIAN UNUSED ARMY

Brody

Lemberg

Zloczow

Jaroslawice

Russian objective.

ELEVENTH ARMY (Erdelli)

SÜDARMEE (4 German, 3 Austrian, 1 Turkish div.)

GALICIA

Dniester

Tarnopol

BRUSILOV'S H.Q.

AUSTRIAN THIRD ARMY

SEVENTH ARMY (Belkovitch)

Brzezany

Zlota Lipa

A U S T R I A – H U N G A R Y

Kalusz

Halicz

Jezupol

Stanislau

Strypa

Sereth

Zbrucz

Turning flank move.

6 July

EIGHTH ARMY (Kornilov)

AUSTRIAN SEVENTH ARMY

Dniester

Kolomea

Pruth

Czernowitz

RUMANIA

R U S S I A

1 July

— KEY —

Russian armies.

Russian advances.

Extent of main Russian advance 16 July.

Armies of Central Powers.

0   30
Miles

Map 13a

Russia's Final Effort in 1917

Lt. R. and his company were assigned to an Austrian army unit, probably the "Südarmee." This army included also Hungarian cavalry.

"Nusze, 5-12-17. Straw thatched hamlets looked pretty on the slopes..."

(In East Galicia near the Sereth River.) "Nusze, 5-12-17." (See Map M2)

Troops' quarters in the village of Podlipce, July 1917. Soldier in the foreground is holding a dog.

of our men were in the woods and had to be rounded up. Quickly the supply wagons were loaded with ammunition, weapons and tools, and by evening we were ready to proceed with all our vehicles, on the road leading to Podlipce [Map M2]. The moon was bright overhead when our columns marched through mountain canyons down to Podlipce, towards an unknown fate. Past Pluhow we came to an area we already knew, and late at night we reached the village of Slawna where we were able to lie down for a rest. By now we had come closer to the firing line. There were tracks of military trains that took the wounded from the front and transported food and ammunition to it. All night long we heard the rumbling from the front line. We felt the earth reverberating.

The next morning we lay down in the garden, exhausted from lack of sleep, hoping against hope that we could stay here a little while longer. But then came the order to leave (July 2, 1917). I mounted my horse and, together with the battalion commander, Captain Wagner, and the other company leaders (Lieutenants Lohmann, Sander, and First Lieutenant Kallenbach), led the battalion to the front. The situation was critical. The Russians had penetrated the Mogila Hills. The Austrians who had not

been taken prisoner were running for their lives. We were to march toward the Mogila Hills and prevent the Russians from advancing any further by occupying key positions near Zarudzie [Map M2]. As soon as we
left Slawna we got a clearer picture of the situation. Austrian troops were
trying to retreat through smaller canyons. Whipped by their drivers the
horses strained and pulled the wagons with all their might, since shrapnel and shell bursts came quite close at times. We could see clearly the
commotion and the feverish drive with which everyone tried to get out of
the danger zone.

And so we reached the familiar village of Urlow. From here we
were to start our counterattack. The enemy knew very well that we occupied the village and fired one shell after another that splashed not far
from us into the muddy ground. We observed fleeing Austrians and
wounded German machine gunners racing back breathlessly, never once
looking back. Over hillsides Hungarian cavalry were galloping through
undulating cornfields to salvage their cannons from their sites as quickly
as possible. Soon they were coming back with them at a fast trot. Captain
Wagner, the other company commanders, and I moved ahead on horseback on the road to Zarudzie, toward the enemy positions, to reconnoiter.
We didn't see the enemy anywhere. He was either advancing very carefully or he was re-grouping before another attack. No doubt he had already occupied Zarudzie for we observed activity there. That meant we
could no longer take the entrenchments near Zarudzie-Corzilow. It was
too late for that. So we returned to the village, awaiting further orders.
Immediately the 9th Company (Lieutenant Lohmann) was ordered to
advance (on the right) south of Urlow in the Strypa valley; they fanned
out and soon they disappeared in clouds of gunpowder and machine gun
fire. We stayed behind at first as reserves, in a narrow pass of the village.
The medical officer joined us again after giving some encouragement to
several fleeing Austrians and after getting some German shirkers (yes,
we had those too, unfortunately) back in line. Were we ever happy when
we came upon a keg of red wine left behind by the Austrians! This was
just the right thing for the entire company.

One Austrian company, under the command of a cadet, was added
to ours to lend us support. I was rather dubious about them as the cadet
himself told us these were some of the worst soldiers; they had been
pulled out from the front line in order to get more training in Zloczow.
Their Hungarian comrades on the front, unfortunately, had had tough
luck (32nd Austro-Hungarian Infantry Division). While our own III Battalion already had suffered huge losses near Koniuchi [Map M2] due to

the breakdown of Austrian troops, the Hungarian units, who were now occupying our positions near Zarudzie on the Mogila Hills, were mostly taken prisoners, barely escaping complete annihilation. Because of the betrayal by Czech troops [Map 6b] the Russians managed to get behind the lines, and despite desperate counterattacks those brave Hungarians who had survived had to hand over their weapons and be taken prisoner. Even the artillery positions were taken by the enemy in a surprise attack. A German battery in Zarudzie was suddenly confronted by Russians penetrating their line. They escaped with their wounded to Urlow where they were now sitting with us, telling us their story. Of course, they had had to abandon their cannons.

The hours passed and we were still stranded on our slope in the village. I made use of the time by checking out the whereabouts of the Austrian brigade-staff in the village. By chance, I saw the Austrian brigade commander, Colonel Gaksch, sitting on a grassy hillside. I remembered him well from our trenches at Zarudzie. He sat there bent over, giving the impression of a physically and mentally broken man. I could feel for him since I had seen myself how, during the winter months, he had cared with heart and soul for the well-being of his men and for the improvements of the entrenchments. And now all was lost. The 64th Infantry Brigade had fought valiantly with their brave Regiments 6 and 86. For four days they had been exposed to a barrage of fire on the Mogila Hills. Several attacks followed, all of which had been skillfully repelled, the last one with a counterattack. They had still been fighting on the Mogila Hills at two o'clock in the afternoon and had requested barrage-fire from batteries that had already been overrun by the Russians from behind the brave gunners. The fighting of the 64th Infantry Brigade had been exemplary, but now they were taken prisoner because the Czechs had betrayed them.

Finally the command was given to advance. It was by now late afternoon and the summer heat was beating down on the fields as we stooped low while climbing up the hillside behind the village to be protected from enemy view. Along the mountain ridge ran an unusually deep trench that led to an elaborate system of dugouts which served as a salient several hundred meters to the front, as far as the protruding mountain ridge of Za Figura.

One after the other, we jumped through an opening into the trench. Apparently the Russians were still pretty far away, or else they simply had not noticed us because we were not subjected to enemy fire as we jumped into the trench. We had become terribly thirsty, but there was hardly anything to drink. With the help of First Lieutenant Kallenbach,

I now tried to locate on the map those trenches to which the regiment had assigned us and which we were to take over before the Russians penetrated our lines even further. We surveyed the area: To the right of us they were still fighting hard. In front of us was the city of Zborow, partially hidden from view by the Mogila Hills [Map M2]. Our battalion had been in possession of these heights into spring. Now these hills that we had considered invincible were in the hands of the Russians. Even our old Zarudzie, where once our field kitchens used to stop, was for the most part occupied by the Russians. It was frightening to see the Russian artillery fire advance and our entire battle zone moved back to our disadvantage. On the hills to the right of us German skirmishing lines moved forward. For now, I left my company behind and walked with First Lieutenant Kallenbach cautiously through the trenches to the front to learn which way they were going and above all, to make contact with our troops on the left flank. For a long, long time we wandered about, trying to find our way in the deserted trenches until we had finished our task: We had made contact with other German troops to our right and to the left, and then toward evening, we moved both our companies into the vacant space between them. Next, the machine guns were put in place, guards were positioned, and we lay down in the open trench to get some rest, above us the open, starry skies.

The next day we started work on the trenches, a job well-known to us from our days in Jaroslavice. For the moment, the Russian advances had come to a halt, but we had to count on their continuing the offensive soon. There was no rest for us, day or night. This time we had no time to build large dugouts, even less so since there was very little building material. For my own little hideaway I had only a foxhole with three steps leading into it. Inside we put two boards across, on which both my orderly and I slept at night. Our time in this uncovered trench was most uncomfortable since the Russians started to zero in on us with their fire. It was lucky that the heavy-caliber shells fell into the main trench, about 200 meters behind us, where Lieutenant Ewald was with his machine guns. The Russians probably thought that our main contingent was there. Patrol activities were stepped up. Russians were seen in the valley near Korzolow. It seemed they had assembled larger groups of reserves there. We had set up an advanced outpost on the ridge of Za Figura. I walked along the entire length of our defense line and finally reached the hilltop up front, from where I could see down into the valley of Zarudzie and Korzolow. Up here was the advanced outpost of First Lieutenant Kallenbach with his eight men. This is where the command post of the Austrian brigade used to be.

That's why we found a very nice, covered dugout here, protected from gunfire. Several steps led down; the walls were decorated with pictures and picture postcards. Indeed, it was cozy down here. But this outpost was dangerous. It was too far from the main trench and too vulnerable to a Russian surprise attack. I expressed my concerns to Kallenbach, and Lieutenant Peters remarked he, with his sentries, would have no trouble taking Kallenbach prisoner on the spot. We ventured on still further and climbed to the highest point of the mountain ridge. We had now walked more than 1,200 meters away from our main trench towards the enemy. Suddenly two Russians rounded the corner and came closer. Unsuspecting, with mess-kits in hand, they walked forward. We took aim at once which sent them tumbling into a hole. Without a doubt, these were also sentries from an outpost and only about 100 meters away from us.

July 6, 1917: The Battle East of Zloczow

The next few days our artillery was very active. Daily, German and Hungarian artillery observers of many different batteries came to us to find the range of both defensive and offensive fire. We worked feverishly for there was no doubt that we could expect a Russian assault. July 6 was the day of the big battle. Early, around 5:45, we were abruptly awakened because heavy Russian artillery fire had set in. This tested our nerves severely because our dugouts offered only minimal protection. I sat with my orderly on my board in our incomplete trench entrance, watching for a while the heavy caliber shells crashing all around us. Apparently the Russians assumed, as mentioned earlier, that our trenches in the rear represented our major position because their heavy artillery fire was increasingly directed there—200 meters behind us. Shrapnel was bursting above us. Behind us black clouds of smoke rose high and our machine gunners unfortunately had many losses. Hill Za Figura was also the object of heavy gunfire. "What is going to happen to Kallenbach and his sentries?" was our first thought. Later we found out that as early as 6:30, the Russians had succeeded in surrounding Hill Za Figura and had overrun the outpost. First Lieutenant Kallenbach, Lieutenant Draherin and 17 men were taken prisoner. Only three men escaped, one of whom was found later, dead. From our trench we could look into a basin that was enclosed to the right by Hill Za Figura and to the left by another mountain ridge. The background was formed by the impressive Mogila Hill. On its lower left side a few houses of the city of Zborow were visible. At the foot of the Mogila Hill the village Korzolow was half hidden.

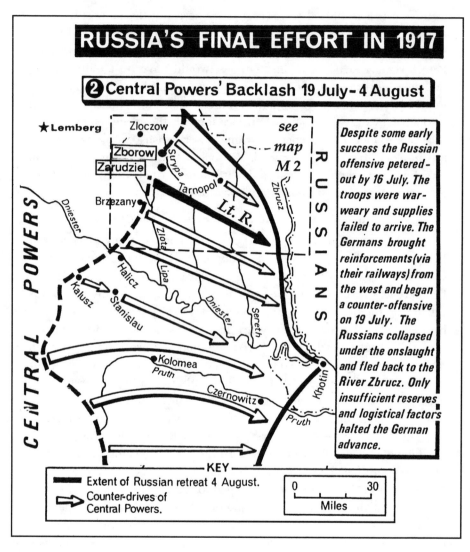

RUSSIA'S FINAL EFFORT IN 1917

❷ Central Powers' Backlash 19 July – 4 August

★ Lemberg

Zloczow

Zborow

Zarudzie

Brzezany

Strypa

Tarnopol

Lt. R.

Zbrucz

see map M 2

RUSSIANS

Dniester

Zlota Lipa

Halicz

Kalusz

Stanislau

Dniester

Sereth

Kolomea

Pruth

Czernowitz

Khotin

Pruth

CENTRAL POWERS

Despite some early success the Russian offensive petered-out by 16 July. The troops were war-weary and supplies failed to arrive. The Germans brought reinforcements (via their railways) from the west and began a counter-offensive on 19 July. The Russians collapsed under the onslaught and fled back to the River Zbrucz. Only insufficient reserves and logistical factors halted the German advance.

— KEY —

▬ Extent of Russian retreat 4 August.

⇨ Counter-drives of Central Powers.

0   30

Miles

Map 13b

Central Powers' Backlash July 19–August 4, 1917

Lt. R.'s regiment took part in the counteroffensive. Major battles were fought between the Strypa and the Zbrucz Rivers. (Includes "Inset" for Map M2.)

At 9:15 in the morning the Russians advanced. We saw them coming from below in perfect open formations, in waves line after line rather than in huge masses, not at all the way it was always claimed in the newspapers. They advanced toward Za Figura and the left hill, Dodeba, where they apparently had covered access routes. This was a stirring, impressive spectacle, the way the enemy moved towards our trenches step by step, but scary beyond words. In our trench we got everything ready for our defense: The machine guns were put in place, ammunition readied in sufficient quantity, and mine and grenade throwers set up. We were most vulnerable in the direction of the Za Figura Hill. A trench led directly from there to our position, thus protecting the Russians from view on their way. I therefore went with some volunteers to our trench exit where we barricaded it with sand bags and wire. My former orderly, Corporal Hennlein, outdid himself in his efforts to be helpful. He faced danger without blinking an eye. Even when I warned him not to be foolhardy, he'd say, "Nothing will happen to me." This time, too, I warned him emphatically. Impulsively he jumped with sandbags across the parapet to secure the trench's opening. When he was about to jump back, he dropped down mortally wounded from a gunshot to his head. We were shaken as we stood by his lifeless body. How many times had we fought side by side, and how many times had his service been extraordinary in difficult circumstances.

All roads leading to our trenches were under very heavy fire, which made it difficult to get back. At that moment some men from the 11th Company dragged Lieutenant Peters on a tarp over to us. Panting and heaving they came up the mountain through the shrapnel fire. Konrad Bohn, his loyal orderly, feared the lieutenant was near death. When Lieutenant Peters had looked across the parapet with his binoculars, he was shot right above his heart. There he was now lying on the tarp, pale as death, still whimpering softly. I walked over to the machine guns. The Russians had already overpowered the Za Figura outpost. We now started sending red flares up from all our different trenches to let our artillery know that we needed their support. The first German shells came flying soon afterwards. On the Za Figura hill the Russians were hurrying across the mountain ridge and jumped into our well-fortified trench up front from which they could approach our defenses, completely covered. Our machine guns pounded into every new wave, and we could see clearly how the Russians ducked, trying hard to avoid the shells. We were extremely nervous.

On our left the Austrians had already retreated. Our artillery increased their fire more and more. Heavy and light trench mortars added to its impact. There was a roaring, cracking, and vibrating fury of unheard proportions, the effect of artillery fire as we had never experienced it before. Soon the dense curtain of fire before us became so thick and heavy that behind it everything gradually disappeared: Za Figura, Mogila, Dodeba, and the entire valley. In the end we saw only lightning flashes of bursting shrapnel and clouds of smoke rising high. There we were standing in our trenches gasping at such an awesome spectacle. We were seized by a feeling of pride, triumph, and power as we stood in the midst of a magic fire. Not even the most fearless warrior would have dared cross this fiery cauldron. The battle had been raging for as long as seven hours, and when evening fell, flames were shooting to the sky from the burning town of Zarudzie, painting a red veil on the clouds of smoke that were hovering over the trenches. From 8:30 to 9:30 in the evening, both artilleries assumed their shooting. Then all was quiet.

On July 7 this defensive battle turned into a less vehement trench warfare, and during the next few days we were able to rest up a bit. The enemy fire died down almost completely so that we were able to resume repairing the trenches, a familiar job for us. But then, on July 12, 1917, it started raining without a pause, thus putting an end to our repairs. For three days and nights water flooded our trenches so that we were absolutely miserable inside. Walking through the trench would have been impossible. Your boots were simply swallowed up by the mud. Soon the food supply stopped because our "food runners" could no longer get through the morass. In my hideaway water dripped down the steps; from above water trickled through the tarp and my bed was swimming in water. For days we sat like this, drenched through and through, until we were finally relieved for a day and managed to find quarters in the village Urlov. We dried our clothes, changed into fresh undergarments and at night our cheerful staff physician treated us to a cup of delicious tea and a good cigar. Finally, on the evening of July 15, the clouds opened up, giving us a glimpse of blue sky. With renewed hope we welcomed the first rays of the sun that began breaking through the clouds in the evening. Our artillery once again sent its heaviest calibers across to the Mogila Hills.

In the meantime the Supreme Command had assembled several divisions around Zloczow. The execution of the big, long-planned counterattack on the Galician front was entrusted to General von Winckler. It was rumored that there were several regiments with a lot of heavy and light artillery in our Mogilka camp. On July 19 the counteroffensive that had been postponed several times, began between Zwyzyn and Hukalowce,

Galician Refugees

as well as on the Zlota Gora and the Wertepi Height. From four to seven
o'clock in the morning enemy positions were to be gassed, then artillery
fire was to precede the attack between 7:10 and 8:45. The breakthrough
attack was to occur at 8:45. It would be our task to pin down the enemy
forces in their trenches and not to exert pressure on the enemy until
given orders to that effect, then fight in coordination with the other troops
near us.

Early on July 19, we did indeed hear the low thunder of cannons
from Wertepi and Zlota Gora. For hours the floor in my dugout was
vibrating from their dull, rolling sound. At 9:15 a telephone call announced
that our troops had taken Zlota Gora by storm, and at 9:25, Wertepi. Our
2nd Battalion had already begun their thrust to the east from there. Our
patrols, too, started exploring. Za Figura was completely cleared of enemy forces. By noon, Zborow and part of the Mogila Hills had been cleared
of enemy troops as well [Map M2]. Now my men jumped out of our
trenches, wire clippers in hand, cutting all wire barricades. We gathered
up our belongings, rifles slung over our shoulders, and laughing and cheer-
ing we moved forward. Around 2:20 the battalion's staff officers moved
down from the hill. "Forward, march!" was the command. From all trenches

Refugees Cooking Noon Meal

long columns started marching forward. Cautiously, we climbed up to the Za Figura Hills. The artillery battle was still raging nearby and the Russians couldn't be further away than a few thousand meters. Curious, I walked with Second Lieutenant Schmidt through the many trenches of the hill. Our former dugout on Za Figura was completely destroyed. A dead Russian lay in one trench, half naked. There still were other signs of combat: Scattered about were rifles and cartridges as well as pieces of clothing. It was here that First Lieutenant Kallenbach had been taken prisoner on July 6. Regimental archives note that the guards were over-powered only after heavy fighting, with 60 Russians killed and after having used up their last round of ammunition.

We looked down into this valley where we had been entrenched for months in the winter of 1916–17. Now, after heavy fighting, it was ours again. To be sure, Zarudzie was reduced to a pile of ashes; the peasants had fled with their few belongings. The church tower had collapsed from a direct hit and the church itself had been damaged severely. Within our view were the Zlota Gora Hills and Wertepi. Column after column of marching soldiers moved across, heading east. To the right of us there were still troops in their trenches, waiting for their marching orders. The artillery kept on shooting.

In wide open formation we now climb down into the Strypa valley where we regroup on a dairy farm. There, a lot of Russians emerge from the barns, running toward us and wanting to be taken prisoner. On the other side of Zarudzie, some Russians still roam the tall wheat fields. By the time we are on the crest of a hill beyond Zarudzie, we receive orders from the battalion to stay put for a while. The weather is wonderful and we lie down in the grass, glad to be able to rest a little. After the cold rainy days in the trenches our limbs have become stiff and rigid and un-used to walking. The village below is crowded with troops. Just now the Hungarian artillery passes through. Since we have more time on hand I walk over to the cemetery. Many crosses for dead soldiers, ours included, are broken and scattered about; the church tower lies in ruins, and the roof of the church is severely damaged. This church and this cemetery hold many memories for us.

Finally, I received orders to lead the battalion that I had taken over back to the dairy farm. That meant we had to return to the same place where earlier we had taken the Russians prisoner. Meanwhile it was get-ting dark. We sat around in groups, enjoying the delicious water from the well. It was around 7 p.m. when we received orders to march across Hills 391 and 383 to Chorobrow [Map M2]. Our 1st and 2nd Battalions were already on their way across the Mogila Hills, and our battalion's staff officers had gone ahead on horseback. We started marching past the Mogila on the right. It was a bumpy trail, in poor condition. In places it had been torn up by deep shell craters. With heavy footsteps we climbed on. We were supposed to march first to a certain place where a bicyclist was to meet us with more detailed information. Slowly the sun was setting and complete darkness enveloped us. It was so dark that we could no longer orient ourselves with our map. I wasn't quite sure whether I had chosen the right path. A few Austrian officers we met on the way were at least able to point us in the general direction. Finally, after a very exhausting march, we actually came upon the bicyclist at the designated place. He reported to us that the staff had already gone ahead to Chorobrow and that we were to follow, but which way he didn't know either.

On the twentieth, at night, our 1st and 2nd Battalions reached the Chorobrow-Chorsciec line. At this point, we stopped for a longer rest because my men were utterly exhausted. The poor machine gunners had to carry their heavy machine guns and ammunition containers themselves, since there were no vehicles accompanying us. It was a Herculean task. But in the end we had to keep moving. Our footpath deteriorated more and more and finally stopped altogether. So we started marching across stubble-fields, with me and Lieutenant Lohmann up front, luminous compass in hand. Far away, the sky was lit by huge fires which told us how far the Russians had already withdrawn. We came closer and closer to the old trenches. They proved to be a serious obstacle since they were several meters deep and the walls went straight down. We couldn't find any steps or entrances anywhere. That meant we had to slide down, very difficult in the dark, by holding on to each other's hands. Under our breath, we handed down backpacks, rifles, machine guns, and ammunition containers, only to pull them back up again on the other side, which was extremely difficult. It took us hours to finally get the whole battalion together on the other side of the trenches.

Then we continued on our march. Now and then we heard someone shout in the darkness. They were orderlies of other battalions. I now headed exactly east toward the fiery glow of a burning village. By all estimates we should now be running into deserted Russian trenches. We struggled forward through shell-scarred, overgrown fields, apparently moving forward alongside trenches. And, sure enough, we finally stumbled over Russian wire barriers. It was probably past midnight. But how were we to get through this maze of barbed wire? We searched for openings; we cut through the wire, but in vain. There were ever new wire entanglements. I realized that it was useless to go on and ordered everyone to stop and get some rest. So we lay in this maze of barbed wire, dead tired and worn out. Shivering, we pulled our coats closer around us. A cold wind came up and rain showers swept over us. I suddenly felt nauseated so that I, for one, couldn't sleep at all.

After the Battle

When morning dawned, I jumped up. Around me everyone was still asleep. The early morning cast its light over the terrain. We were up fairly high. Right away I pulled out my map and compass. Was I ever happy when I saw in the valley below the peaceful village of Chorobrow. Only a few steps away from where we had stopped was the path that led through the wire down into the valley. That meant that the night before we had, without maps, stayed on course despite that darkness. We got ready in a hurry, and by 5:30 in the morning we were crossing the Russian trenches on our way down into the valley. We came through inhospitable areas. The fields were not cultivated as they are back home. Crowds of peasants were sifting through the debris in the trenches to salvage household items, boards, and beams. Although we were famished we walked on into the morning in good spirits, looking forward to a good rest in nearby Chorobrow, to fill our stomachs and warm our frozen bodies with a hot drink.

By 5 p.m. on July 21, 1917, we marched into the village. It was a miserable place. Since it was so close behind the front, it had suffered greatly from all the combat activity. Most of its residents had fled. When he saw us from a distance, our battalion commander welcomed us with a loud hurrah. Was he ever glad to have his battalion back! We gathered some straw to use on the damp ground and tried to get some sleep. It wasn't until the sun came up and we had had a cup of hot coffee that we felt warm again and our mood improved. But as usual there was no time for a longer rest. Around eight o'clock we were alerted to march at 8:30. You could hear our good men sighing and cursing, but we fell in on time, and off we marched toward Glinna. I still didn't feel very good but was back on my feet as soon as our good staff-physician handed me a strong shot of Schnapps. All company commanders were now together again. At the head of our battalion and with the battalion's staff, we happily forged ahead on horseback. None of the fields were cultivated here, only a few miserable weeds covered the soil; here and there a dead horse lay on the ground which was cratered with shell holes. At first there were no more Russians in sight; they had left, moving east. Not until we came to the village of Glinna did an unexploded shell suddenly drop nearby [Map M2].

The regiment's adjutant, Lieutenant Thomas, approaches us on horseback to transmit further orders. Immediately we turn right into the road leading up the hill of the Kamienna Gora. Each company is marching in closed formation, but then they spread out in wide skirmishing order. Off and on we see the telltale little clouds of shrapnel. Finally we reach the top of the hill. A substantial trench stretches all along its ridge. I jump down into it, exchange a few words with the battalion commander of the 2nd Battalion, Captain Rasch, and then we are off again. Others jump into the trench when suddenly there is a roar in the air and a crash, and two of my best men lie dead on the very spot where I had just left.

We finally reached a farmhouse from where we could see, several kilometers away, innumerable small dots in many rows: our advancing troops. Long trenches encircled the heights but had already been crossed by our troops. In the distance we could still see Russians retreating. Gigantic fiery columns and enormous clouds shaped like mushrooms were rising high, probably the result of explosions. Enemy artillery was still affecting us, especially the left wing of our battalion. We had a hard time crossing the stubble fields, mountains and valleys, gorges and trenches. But we kept going all through these difficult, very fatiguing days. Not a single soldier stayed behind. The good feeling of having escaped the worst danger at least for a while, the victories of the last few days that lifted our spirits, and last but not least our hope to crush the opponent soon and for good—all this revived us in mind and body.

But hunger began gnawing at us. We had only a few pieces of left-over bread to sustain us since the field kitchens were still far away. All day yesterday we had had nothing warm to eat, and it was at the very least questionable whether we would get anything today. At least we were finally able to march in closed formation again and on a fairly good path through the fields. There were no Russians anywhere. The sun was beating down on us relentlessly and we grew more weary all the time. At last, to our great delight, the field kitchens came in our direction just as we were approaching Kaplince. We sat down under a linden tree, on stone walls and slopes, enjoying some wonderful pea soup. Bone-tired, we then stretched out under green trees for a refreshing slumber until our marching orders arrived. The enemy had vanished and we marched undisturbed as far as the village of Budylow [Map M2] where we arrived around five o'clock in the evening. The place was full of soldiers. Austrian companies had already arrived and were fanning out up the hillsides. Our two other battalions and the regiment's staff were already in the village. With all these troops, there simply weren't enough houses to provide quarter for us all. Therefore—it was already late at night—we set up tents and bivouacked there.

We were overjoyed to welcome back Lieutenant Peters, who had been severely wounded when we were engaged in a defensive battle in East Galicia [July 1, 1917]. After a short stay in a field hospital and with the bullet still in his body, he had returned to his troops even though he was far from recovered. This showed once again how many an officer was truly dedicated, devoted to his troops, preferring to share their hardships, even death, rather than shirk his duties by staying cowardly behind the lines.

This night we had only a short rest. It was still dark when we broke camp. We barely had time to gulp down some hot coffee before we were off again. The companies were marching separately. The sun was just coming up when we stopped for the first time. Tall wooden crosses lined the roads where Ruthenian peasants, men and women, were kneeling and praying, covering the cross with their kisses. We witnessed such scenes frequently! [Ruthenian=Ukrainian.]

We continued east through tall fields of grain, reaching Horodyseze around noon. There the entire Regiment 32 was already assembled at the foot of a mountain by a little river. The staff was standing on Hill 367 to

Roadside shrine (?) with wooden crosses lining the street. Red Cross soldier in center.

Greek Orthodox Church

Interior of a Greek Orthodox Church

The sanctuary is adorned with fresh flowers.

survey the situation. Our regiment was now taken out of the front line to follow the Unit Wilhelmi as support group, along with 2 howitzer and field-cannon batteries, Storm Company 13, and a sharpshooter section. At first we were to cover the right flank of the group until the Beskiden Corps [Austrian unit] would catch up with us. The avant-garde of this corps arrived as early as eight o'clock in the morning, but we didn't leave until four in the afternoon. This gave us several more hours for relaxation here. It was a very nice afternoon, sunny and warm, and soon almost the entire battalion was swimming in the cool waters of the river. Black clouds of smoke were still rising from the railroad station at Denysow. The enemy was not very far away. A cavalry unit returned with a wounded horse, its rider lost. We marched past a large Russian supply depot near the railroad station of Denysow. Many troops took along supplies of canned goods, dried fish, etc.

Unfortunately we had to hurry past and entered once again desolate areas where the war had raged years ago, areas that had been completely abandoned by the people and where not a single field had seen a plough. [The German military map M2 shows several dates when battles were fought there in 1915.] As far as the eye could see, the fields were covered with weeds, a vast, terribly barren landscape. We walked through an utterly deserted village. Not a sound came from the deserted houses. Once there must have been the German front here. On some houses there were still signs in German, such as *Gasraum* [Detox Center], *Entlausungsanstalt* [Delousing Center], and others. Seemingly interminable trenches crossed the terrain and row upon row of wire barricades protruded above the tall weeds. Our march was long and cumbersome. A dry wind swept across the wasteland, parching our throats. When a fine drizzle started towards evening I felt nauseated again. I therefore got off my horse and continued on foot. Finally, towards nine o'clock in the evening, when it was getting dark, we bivouacked near Jozefowka that was totally destroyed and completely deserted (July 22, 1917). I was lying on the ground wrapped in my coat when the staff physician, helpful as always, crawled into my tent bringing me a tonic.

Our departure was set for very early in the morning. The Russians were quite close. The object of the fight was Hill 340. Since we were the reserves, we stayed north of Hill 340 until the enemy was beaten back. Then we marched on. Soon we were near the Sereth River [Map M2]; its crossings were the object of heavy fighting further north. After having broken camp in Zazdrocz on July 23, our division with baggage trains and horses was crawling along on deserted roads, when we were targeted by strong artillery fire. That forced us to seek refuge in a sheltered basin where the Russians could no longer see us. They were watching us from the wooded hills above. With strong machine gun fire they succeeded in stopping the Imperial Infantry Regiment 70, even though our batteries were firing with all their might. The 51 Corps advanced in another area, and the Russians retreated towards the road linking Strusow-Ziclona-Kascyma. At this point, our 197th Infantry Division was to relieve the 237th Infantry Division and secure the bridgehead between Zahami and Podhajczyki-Justinowce, occupied by the 244th Infantry Brigade [Map M2]. But at first, our battalion spent almost all afternoon in a garden in Bernadowka. It was a gorgeous summer day and we were able to get a good rest. What did we care that shrapnel exploded on the road not far from us, at the edge of the forest? Later all was quiet again, and at 8 p.m. we left. A destroyed Russian armored car with machine guns and artillery as well as several dead horses were lying alongside the road. It was pitchdark when we literally had to grope our way forward. But we were in an upbeat mood. Together with Vadding, the battalion commander, and Lieutenant Dubuisson, we four company commanders rode along joking and laughing, humming one melody after another, until we finally made camp at the foot of Hill 341, southeast of Olendry at 11:30 at night.

Fierce battles had again taken place not far from here. When we marched on the next morning we came through a field covered with corpses. Large numbers of Russian rifles with bayonets were stuck in the ground, and the dead Russians looked at us with a blank and cold stare. They were lying all over the fields of Srednie Garby and the dairy farm of Wybranowka. We were relieved finally to get away from this gruesome sight. At night we camped near Wybranowka. The 197th Infantry Division had just been detached from its former unit to be placed under the command of the army of Count Bothmer (Beskiden Corps) [Beskiden = Region in the West Carpathian mountains] along with the 237th Infantry Division. The next morning we received orders that our reserve division was to march to Podhajgyki-Justynowce via Church 329 and Church 322, then continue to Janow [Map M2]. Leading there was a nice country road from where we had a scenic view of Podhajczyk and the Sereth valley [Map M2], and which took us through nice wooded areas. It had been a beautiful day when at night we pitched our tents and, with our staff physician and Lieutenant Peters, had the pleasure of eating a chicken, all the while engaged in lively conversation. Tired out, we then stretched out inside our tent only to be awakened after a very short rest around 12:30 a.m.; by 1:30 we were on the road again.

It was July 27, 1917. Lighting the way with flashlights, the infantry crossed the Sereth River, walking in single file over a quickly erected makeshift bridge. All vehicles drove through the water. Gradually it got light and we marched through the beautiful Sereth valley via Deremowka to Za Gora where we bivouacked, around five o'clock in the morning. There we learned (Lieutenant Neese) that the Russians had put three new divisions into action. But the word was said that discipline among the Russian troops had suffered greatly. After the short night rest and the long night march (25 kilometers) we were quite fatigued and hungry, but the field kitchen didn't arrive until five o'clock in the evening. We were to join the I/L 32 [Infantry Landwehr 32] and had to march on the double to catch up with them on the way to Hill 341 via Woligory (Chorostkow) [Map M2], where we bivouacked. Soon we were on our way east again across the railroad tracks. At this point our company separated from the 1st and 3rd Battalion, and we marched toward Celejow. It was a lovely evening as we were moving quietly through rich wheatfields, looking forward to quarters nearby. Our acting quarter officer Weber and Second Lieutenant Eschenbach had gone ahead to find quarters for us when, all of a sudden, they came riding back across the hill, out of breath, shouting from the distance, "Cossacks are in the village." After a brief consultation with Vadding, we decided to move on in open formation, taking all necessary precautions. It was already getting dark when we approached the village. There was no sign of the Cossacks; they had left, knowing we were coming. They were now in the forest east of Celejow. I continued marching with my company as far as Liczkowze where, in total darkness, I set up guards and sentries to make sure we were safe.

When I entered the village at the head of my company, we were immediately surrounded by jubilant villagers. A young man named Nikolaus, who had worked in Germany and knew German, called out, "Thank God you made it. At last, at last we are rid of the Russians." He could hardly contain himself for joy, kissed my hand and almost embraced me, he was so elated. And when I finally lay down on my bed of straw— way past midnight—my hosts, simple peasants, still put some milk, bread, and cheese for me on the table.

We were very close to the enemy. In several places our infantry screen had met with enemy resistance. But that was soon broken by our artillery fire. Our march on July 28 was going in the direction of the church tower of Olchowce [near Husiatyn, Map M2] with the II Battalion once again at the head while our III stayed initially in staggered formation on the left side to cover the left flanks, until the 244th Infantry Brigade linked up with our regiment. We came across a number of rearguards and dispersed them, especially near Czabarowka where there was strong resistance. Forty deserters and 18 prisoners were taken.

As early as six o'clock we were on our march again. We had received our orders so late that we couldn't make the designated meeting place on time, which earned us a severe reprimand. Soon we were past Nizborg Stare on a path taking us through beautiful wheatfields. Nestled amidst green bushes and trees, picture pretty dairy farms. How vast and fertile this land was! To the right of us we saw the two other battalions of our regiment moving on: the ones whose left flank we were to cover. We found Hill 313, which controlled the whole area, free from the enemy. We advanced in skirmishing order, but, behind the hill we were able to proceed together again. Now we were getting closer and closer to the Russian border river, Zbrucz, that was 10-15 meters wide and rather deep.

The Battle for Hill 306 near the Zbrucz River [Map M2]

Beyond the river with its steep shoreline, the terrain rises terrace-like to Hill 306. Taking that hill is the target. Up there the Russians have dug in, determined to resist in a desperate last ditch effort. When Hill 313 lies behind us, the first infantry bullets whizz around our heads. Corporal Völker, 10/L 32, is fatally wounded. The 11th Company is sent to Tribuchowce to secure the area; the 9th and 10th Companies are now under orders of the regiment's staff, and my 12th Company under the Second Battalion 32. The Russians cover all roads and pathways where we are marching with heavy artillery fire; as a result supply vehicles lag behind. Across hilltops and through valleys we keep to the right in single file and far apart; even so we are targeted by single, hard hitting shells. Tall grain fields nearby offer some protection; at last, the hills of Zbrucz come into view.

An imposing battlefield unfolds before our eyes: Below, by the Zbrucz River, rifle fire is cracking and field artillery thundering. The village of Olchowce is the focus of heavy artillery fire and is shrouded in clouds of smoke. A veritable conflagration of fire and flashes of lightning burst through the gun smoke. At this point, the Germans start their offensive across the wide open fields. I am still on horseback but will now have to send my horse back to the river. I have to find the battalion's staff. They are supposed to be further down in the fields. I work my way through thick fields of grain and finally find Vadding, after much searching and shouting. He gives me my orders at once. I am to join the Second Battalion and advance with my company on the road toward Olchowce. The gunfire is intensifying and becoming more bothersome; by the time we reach the highway, it is as if a hail of fire is raining down on the street. It feels like the end for us. I cower behind the Saint's Statue (#271) in order to find some shelter behind its masonry. Two officers are hiding there already. They are from the next division on our left (Division 237). Their front unit has reached this point only a little while ago, while the rest of their division is still far behind. This means that our left wing is isolated and cannot expect any assistance.

My men seek shelter in the trenches on both sides of the road. One soldier next to me is hit. The village of Olchowce, that we are expected to take, is under heavy shrapnel fire. The village of Husiatyn [Map M2], on the Zbrucz River, goes up in flames. It is a ghastly sight: the glaringly bright flames against the sinister walls of smoke that rise to the sky, black as ink. A severe thunderstorm is approaching and its muffled, rolling sound becomes one with the roar of the heavy guns. Zigzagging flashes of lightning come down on the black hills of Zbrucz and, for seconds, light up the dark landscape. In the meantime, we manage to jump forward a few hundred meters, but are now being showered with such strong machine gun fire that the only way out is to lie down in the field amid the tall grain and stay there, motionless, so that the Russians cannot see us and will stop shooting. The moment we raise our heads, bullets whiz past us. We can move neither forward nor backward. In addition, a massive thunderstorm is breaking loose and drenching us to the bone. We may have been there for more than an hour when roaring above our heads, there follows a tremendous German bombardment of the Russian positions. That is the right moment for us to proceed. A piercing tone from my signal-whistle and off we are, running toward the village through hedges and gardens till we get to a dairy farm.

It had been hell to see the Russian shells come down earlier. Now things had quieted down. We were glad we had gotten this far. Some of my men were already in the farmhouse, and to my great surprise, whom did I see? Lieutenant Nille from the II Battalion. At considerable speed, he had managed to get here before the onset of heavy fire, had passed a few dangerous hours and now, sitting at a table, enjoyed good and plentiful food. The owner himself played host! I couldn't imagine anything better than to join in, after lying in rain and mud for hours. We relished an excellent pork roast and a few cups of Russian tea. Even the continued artillery battle outside could not rob us of our temporary contentment. Since I had not yet received any further orders for my company, I had my men served some tea also while I visited the wounded that lay in one of the rooms in the farmhouse.

The Russians were only a few hundred meters away on the hills on
the other side of the Zbrucz River. Lieutenant Nille had posted a large
number of sentries and guards down by the river so that we were safe on
this side. Gradually the house was filled with officers. The entire staff of
the II Battalion 32 (Colonel Rasch) settled in here, and now there was a
lot of commotion and restlessness, all the more so because it looked like
more battle action the next day. Meanwhile, I had inspected the village
and acquainted myself with the terrain. I also reinforced the outposts
with men from my company. Rifle shots were popping and exploding
everywhere. We weren't safe anywhere. Darkness had slowly set in and
we were expecting the field kitchen. But it never came. Although I was
dead tired, I managed to get out in the dark and search for my third
platoon that had advanced further south of Olchowce under Lieutenant
Sander and was supposed to be near a cemetery. Following a long and
risky search, I found him at last and took the whole platoon back to the
farmhouse where we had a few hours of restless sleep.

On July 21, 1917, we are up early in the morning. Colonel Rasch
takes the company leaders with him into the village, where—protected
by a stone wall—he gives us detailed orders for the day. Hill 306 is to be
taken and we are to do it proceeding from our present location at Olchowce.
We are to storm the hill at 9:30 a.m. Our artillery starts shooting, but
then the attack is postponed to 10:30, then to 11:30 and 12:30. At 12:15
our attack is canceled because the Russians are advancing approximately
800 meters to the left of II/L 32. Apparently our campaign is now suffering from poor preparation and lack of leadership. We are always late in
receiving our orders!

As a result my troops and I had already set out for the attack in the
morning. We tried to get across the creek to reach Hill 306. Lieutenant
Nille with his troops was located nearby. No matter where you walked in
the village, the Russians would detect you and shoot from their positions
higher up. That's how I lost one of my best men, Private Rodemann,
through a direct hit to his throat as he was standing in front of a door of
one of the houses. At last we reached the river bank, ready to cross over.
It was a dangerous maneuver because the creek was well covered by machine gun fire. The moment we showed ourselves, the bullets came flying.
I was the first to take a big leap across, then I squatted down by the road
and leaned against an embankment for protection where the shots whizzed
by above my head. The next man jumped but didn't reach me since he was
felled by a shot to the head. The next one didn't make it either; bullets hit
his throat and leg, wounding him severely. It was a pitiful sight, blood

running down from his mouth and nose. Defying death, the medic—a sergeant—jumped after him and bandaged him as best he could. Machine gun fire rattled above our heads, hitting the hard surface of the road like a downpour. Even grenades came flying at this point.

I was now completely cut off from my company, for in this fire it would have been foolhardy to try to jump back to reach them. The situation became even worse when suddenly the skies opened. Soon I literally swam in water that came rushing down from the slopes. But I stayed glued to my spot, for only a slight move of my head caused the Russians to take note. Finally the sun broke through the clouds again. I had to make a decision. I decided to crawl backwards to the river bank and tried to jump back. Again it was a leap for life or death! The minute the Russians noticed me, they directed their fire all along the riverbank. I slipped and hit the water. My last moment seemed to have come. With all the strength I could muster, I wriggled back to my hiding place, getting set for another jump. One leap! And I literally flew into the arms of my men who were standing on the other side.

I managed to get my men into houses and went myself to Lieutenant Nille who was staying in a barn where he had a telephone connection. Here I had at least a chance to dry my clothes in the sun. By now it was afternoon and my men and I had not had a bite to eat all day. There was no way the field kitchen would be able to reach us. Therefore I went out to search for some food. I made my way behind hedges and bushes so as not to be seen by the Russians and finally slipped into a house. The door was locked, but I forced it open and, to my great joy, found a big pitcher of milk and some bread which we consumed with pleasure and then stretched out on the benches to get some rest after the exertions of this day. However, we weren't safe here either because the entire village was hit by artillery fire again and again.

Finally, the order was given to begin the offensive for Hill 306 at eight p.m. In the meantime, a makeshift footbridge had been constructed near Konhumaz, further south. The Jäger Battalion 25 and the III/L 32, after that the II/L 32 and half of the 1st Battalion, succeeded in getting to the bank on the other side by using this crossing and to take the first line of trenches on the first try, despite very heavy counterattack. All of the Russian counterattacks failed! But our troops had to come to a halt halfway up the hill, in shallow Russian trenches, which offered little protection. Our own losses were heavy: more than 30 dead and 95 wounded. Defying death, Lieutenant Peters crossed the narrow bridge under a hail of fire, only to collapse afterwards from overexertion. A bullet to the head took the life of Lieutenant Franz, the one who had always been so cheerful; and Lieutenant Lohmann sustained a severe head injury when he was hit by an explosive. Everything was done in great haste; commands didn't come until the artillery had already started the offensive. Barely had the companies received orders when the artillery fire ceased again. This resulted in a lull during which the Russians were able to regroup. To be sure, our artillery resumed the attack with all their fire power, but they didn't hit the Russian trenches, whereas the Russians sent one direct hit after another.

We tried to get through to Hill 306 from Kuzminczyk while the other divisions of our company were fighting near Konhumaz. Dusk was setting in as we passed the houses of the village. Using my fieldglasses, I tried to find our contact troops but was unable to detect any forward movement. It was obvious to me that our entire assault on this side of the hill had collapsed once again. It was also clear to me that from this side we would never be able to get up these hillsides even with the largest number of troops, because the Russians put up a tough defense. I told my tired and hungry company to stop and rest a while. We were truly at the end of our rope. In one of the small houses I lay down on some straw, but just when my tired bones had succumbed to a heavy sleep, I was rudely awakened.

First Lieutenant Eckstein from the 1st Battalion had come to relieve me, bringing orders for me to leave with my company for Konhumaz at once to receive further instructions. I suppressed a loud curse. It wasn't easy to get our emaciated bodies moving again. Like robots we inched our way forward in the dark. Only the old sense of duty kept us soldiers going. The dangerous path was pitchdark and we had trouble finding it, keeping alongside the village and constantly subjected to enemy fire. Finally we came close to the Zbrucz River and the enemy's trenches. I found our battalion's staff, Lieutenant Vadding, and his adjutant, Lieutenant Dubuisson, squatting under a bridge. I was given orders: my company was to occupy a section on the other side of the river where earlier an unmanned gap had developed in a Russian trench that had been taken by other companies. I had my company stop in order to orient myself first and, above all, to locate the bridge hastily constructed by our combat engineers. It was pitchdark as I walked alone along the river on a miserable, gravelly path. And then wild artillery fire set in, but I was so exhausted and my senses numb that I was no longer capable of feeling any danger. I was surrounded by the sights and sounds of gunfire. At last I found the bridge; it was actually only a trestle without a railing, with wooden planks to walk on. On the way I ran into Lieutenant Rosenthal who was the orderly from the division's staff, and who was also out to survey the situation. The next day I learned that he had died in action at this site. I went back to get my company. It is still a mystery to me how my men managed to get across this plank bridge with their heavy gear and machine guns.

At dawn we climbed up the steep hillside protected by heavy fog. All was quiet now. As we reached the top, a bright sun rose behind the hillside and bathed us all in its soothing warmth. I jumped into a trench, found a corner and fell asleep at once. Nature demanded its due, regardless of what might happen next. Unspeakably tired and exhausted as we were, sleep had to help us forget all suffering and hardships and give us renewed courage and vigor. When I woke, I examined our situation more closely. We were in an abandoned Russian trench which in front (for us the wrong one) was poorly covered with logs and thus would not protect us from artillery fire. Before us was Hill 306, behind us a steep mountainside, and far below in the valley the Zbrucz River and the small town of Husiatyn [Map M2].

By crossing the river we had driven a deep wedge into the Russian lines so that now we were vulnerable not only in front but also on one side, possibly even in back. There had been no food supply for some time now. The field kitchen had stopped providing us with food the day before yesterday. A redhot sun burned down on us. We suffered from extreme thirst and there was no way of getting any water. Besides, many of us suffered from diarrhea after having eaten green potatoes. At two o'clock we received new orders to attack. That resulted in wild shooting on all sides. Orders went back and forth, often too late, so that we were unable to coordinate our attack with the other companies. We did advance, only to be thrown back into our trenches by heavy grenade fire. This happened again around five in the afternoon and again around nine p.m. We had heavy casualties. Large numbers of wounded were constantly moving through our trench. A direct hit separated Lieutenant Kluglein's head from his body. Our horror-stricken men were thrown to the ground by some ferocious force. Especially the 9th Company had suffered great losses: 39 dead and 120 wounded in one day. It was still extremely hot in the morning of July 31, and the fighting continued. A renewed barrage from our side began at nine in the morning, again with the same bad luck, so that the storming of Hill 306 had to be shelved.

There was barely a moment's rest for us all day long. We tried to repair our trenches that had taken such a beating. We replenished the ammunition and kept working like this until evening. By then we hoped that the day's work was behind us and we lay down on the ground, tired and hungry. Our underwear was soaking wet from sweat, the uniforms grey with dust and dirt. Beside me lay the young Lieutenant Ewald. He declared that since everything seemed to have calmed down at this point, we had once again arrived in heaven, straight out of hell. So we lay there quietly staring into the cloudless sky. In between we did take note of the enemy or glance down into the valley of the Zbrucz River. And then we noticed a few Germans crossing the plank bridge. They were met with shrapnel.

All of a sudden the Russians started a heavy artillery fire. It was around 6:30 p.m. This soon intensified to an earthshaking barrage. German reinforcements were approaching. It was a grandiose spectacle. Our troops arrived in far-flung skirmishing order. We watched as the shells came crashing down into their ranks, roaring and howling. We saw the troops disperse and hit the ground and huge pillars of smoke rise to the sky, shrouding valley and mountains in a thick veil of smoke. With a thunderous noise the shells crashed into the field hospital in Kierniczki where our staff physician, Dr. Trier, worked around the clock despite the constant danger. Our own situation became worse and worse. Gunshots zeroed in on us from every direction. Our breast-work burst apart. Shrapnel was dancing all around us and forced us to seek shelter at another breast-work. But here we couldn't stay very long either. A shell came crashing down on top and caused a whole section of the trench to collapse. It was absolute hell. We had given up all hope for survival and crouched miserably in a corner, expecting the end to come. We dared not stir, for a hail of bullets came clashing against the walls. Finally, when the Russians began the major thrust of their assault, we threw ourselves with our machine guns frantically on top of the parapet, and soon our rifles discharged their bullets with ear-splitting noise. The Russian troops did not get far. We had turned the tide. Their attack was thwarted. This time, we really looked forward to some undisturbed rest. We had completely exhausted ourselves and hunger was still gnawing at us. The field kitchen had still not been able to get near us. There was talk of relief but nothing was definite.

It was a still, beautiful star-lit night. I lay in my corner, tired and numb. There was now complete silence around me. Then, suddenly, someone called my name from the edge of the trench. Was I happy to recognize our field kitchen chef, Max Derbsch. He handed me something to eat and, as a special treat, a small cooked chicken! And now the company food

Lt. R. and his two orderlies were staying with these friendly Galicians after the last battles in August 1917. The sign to the left of the doorway reads: "Lt. Company Commander, E. Rosenhainer. Co. L2, '32." Lt. R. wrote on the back of photo: "To the left of the doorway, my orderly, Albin Waider. To the right, orderly Geilert."

In East Galicia, August–September 1917, during harvest time. Lt. Ernst Rosenhainer in center.

runners arrived also. What a relief it was after days of going hungry, and when we had finally finished our meal after midnight, we lay down to sleep, satisfied. I had hardly put my head down when I was suddenly awakened again: A lieutenant from the 15th Reserve Infantry Division had come with the news that we would be relieved at once. Other companies were standing ready to take our place, he said. We were quick to pack up and leave. No disturbance marred our departure. And when we got closer to the village of Czabarowka [Map M2] we could not see much anymore of the faraway Hill 306 in all that smoke and haze. The battle remained undecided since the forces on both sides were evenly matched, which precluded a victory for either side. Of the entire campaign, these past days had probably been the hardest for me.

A few days of rest helped us recuperate from the heavy fighting. On August 7, 1917, we were given our marching orders. We were to do trench work with the Infantry Division 237 near the Lysa Gora River in the area of Uwisla. That meant we were no longer involved in bigger campaigns. Our 197th Infantry Division was transferred to the area east of Trembowla, and with it our regiment. In the evening of August 16, I arrived with my 12th Company at the outlying trenches of Poplawy. The

German position was pretty far removed from that of the Russians, which was approximately six to seven kilometers away. But our outlying trenches were far out front within the chain of outposts, well over half an hour on foot to the Russian position. We had only a rather thin main front line. All the more lively was the activity of our outposts and patrols in the foremost front area. It was my task to take the command of a larger area of outposts. Every day we would ride into the front area towards the Russians, just to keep active. The enemy's battle activity was limited to moderate shelling and dropping a few bombs from their planes on the villages on our side, and also on our trenches.

Those were good times for us. The fields were ready for harvesting, which we did in order to pass the grain on to the troops and to the people

Friendships Were Formed to Last a Lifetime

On the back of photo: "For Lt. Rosenhainer in fond memory, from Lt. Hentzenroeder. Galicia, October, 1917."

The personal note on the front of this picture reads: "To my dear friend, Rosenhainer, in fond memory, your loyal friend, J.D. [Dubuisson]." (In later years my father frequently mentioned his good friend Dubuisson.)

who lived there. In addition, we continued improving the trenches and used the remaining time for further training of our troops. It was great to be able to socialize in our spare time. I often got together with Lieutenant Dubuisson, the staff physician, Dr. Trier, a jovial man from Cologne, and with other officers from the battalion. Many a friendship was formed here that was to continue through years to come.

In November 1917, the Soviets in Russia began their reign under their leader, Lenin. People were so sick of war over there that individual Russian units at the front independently negotiated a truce with the German troops opposite them. This was the case with our division, too, where Russian delegates arrived for this purpose. Since a peace agreement with Russia seemed near, more and more young German troops were transferred to the Western Front. On December 1, our regiment was detached from the 197th Infantry Division and joined the 92nd Infantry Division under His Excellency Melior. Our former Division Commander, His Exc. Wilhelmi, was visibly moved when, in Trembowla [Map M2], he took leave from his brave troops.

Note: Apparently the author stopped writing his wartime journal at this point although he remained in military service at the front all through the war. He did not return to his home in Neustrelitz (North Germany) to continue his teaching career until February 1919, after having spent additional time on assignments in East Galicia and with combat and occupation forces in the Ukraine.

I.R.H.

Postscript

Operations in the Ukraine

Few details have been available about specific events involving the German military in the Ukraine after it declared its independence from Russia following the Russian revolution in November 1917. Archival records I obtained from the Military History Research Institute in Potsdam, Germany, reveal the following:

Of the 31 divisions and 3 cavalry divisions that remained on the Eastern Front, 13 divisions and all 3 cavalry divisions were sent into the Ukraine in support of the newly established republic. Its rich agricultural lands were important to both Austria and Germany. In fact, to fulfill the demand set forth in the separate peace treaty between the Ukraine and the central allies, the Ukraine was to make shipments of grain and feed to Germany and Austria. However, roving bands of Russian revolutionaries created havoc in the countryside and threatened future harvests.

On February 15, 1918, the new national government of the Ukraine, the "Rada," sent this message to Berlin: "We are asking for assistance in the difficult battle for our very existence....The German army to the west of our northern enemy [i.e., Russia] is strong enough to help us and by intervening can protect our northern border from further aggression by the enemy." It appears that their own Ukrainian troops were unable to stabilize the situation. The Rada government had already retreated from Kiev, the capital of the Ukraine, to the country's western border.

On February 18 German troops marched into Kiev. The goal of the military under General Alexander von Linsingen was to secure major cities and railroad lines. Neutral Russian troops under demobilization orders were not to be attacked, only gangs of revolutionaries.

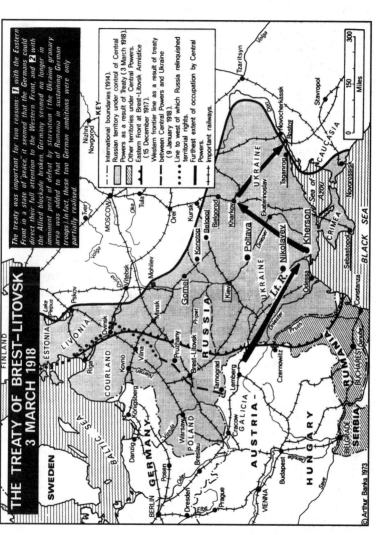

THE TREATY OF BREST-LITOVSK
3 MARCH 1918

The treaty was important for two reasons: **1** with the Eastern Front in a state of 'peace', it seemed that the Germans could direct their full attention to the Western Front, and **2** with the Allied blockade broken, Germany seemed no longer in imminent peril of defeat by starvation (the Ukraine granary area was added to that of Rumania in sustaining German troops). In fact, these two German ambitions were only partially realised.

KEY

– · – · — International boundaries (1914).

⬚ Russian territory under control of Central Powers as a result of Treaty (3 March 1918).

▨ Other territories under Central Powers.

⊣⊢ Eastern Front at Brest-Litovsk Armistice (15 December 1917).

— · — Western frontier line as a result of treaty between Central Powers and Ukraine (9 January 1918).

· · · · · · Line to west of which Russia relinquished territorial rights.

━━━ Furthest extent of occupation by Central Powers.

┼─┼─┼ Important railways.

© Arthur Banks 1973

Map 14

The Treaty of Brest-Litovsk, March 3, 1918

On March 3, 1918, plagued by roving gangs of revolutionaries, the Ukraine called upon German and Austro-Hungarian troops to come and restore order. Lt. R. participated in these maneuvers between February 24 and June 21. All major cities (underlined) were in the hands of the military by that time.

Ultimately the German forces were split into the following three branches: The section north of Kiev under General Gronau was to prevent trains from entering Russian territory; the center section around Kiev under General Groener was to take control of the area around Poltava, the rich granary southeast of Kiev as well as of the industries near Kharkov in the east; and the southern section, Korps Knoerzer, was to take possession of the port cities on the Black Sea.

As officer in the 92 Infantry Division, I Army Corps, my father was part of the southern section. All groups used the existing railroads whenever possible to reach their particular areas.

Since Austro-Hungarian troops arrived from Rumania and were ordered to take the port of Odessa, my father's unit under General Knoerzer was diverted to the south and north of the city. "It is important to reach Nikolayev soon," was the directive sent from the Supreme Command. Odessa was taken three days later as were the other port cities.

Records indicate that the I Army Corps was then diverted northeast to the area near Kharkow, mostly on foot because much of the railroad line had been destroyed. The Russian Bolshevic government in the meantime cast a wary eye on these military operations along their southern border, objecting to any further encroachment. It was therefore determined to concentrate on securing the railroad lines leading into Russia, east and north of Kharkov.

By mid-April most objectives of the three sections—those in the north, in the center, and in the south—had been achieved, often after long battles with Bolshevic troops.

After some administrative dispute, the two occupying powers, Germany and Austria-Hungary, agreed to rule separately, i.e., "each party is to govern absolutely in its own territory in consensus with the Ukrainian government." Austria-Hungary was to administer the southwestern areas of the Ukraine; Germany the rest, including the Crimean peninsula. The valuable coal and mineral rich region near Ekaterinoslav was to be administered by both parties.

In late April the I Army Corps, possibly including my father's 92 I.D., was to leave the Kharkov area and take a hold of the eastern section of the railroad line, Rostov-Moscow. Heavy fighting ensued. However, on May 12 the Bolshevic troops in this area surrendered.

My father's 92 I.D. became part of the occupation forces in the "hinterland," supported by the 1st Cavalry Division, 8th Army, whose main objective was to help with the requisitioning, for payment, of any future crops.

Meantime, combat activities had by no means ceased in all areas, but by mid-June major military operations ceased except for "mop-up" operations necessitated by large and armed Bolshevic troops. In these my father's division participated as needed. His tour of duty in the Ukraine did not end until January 1919. He was discharged in Neustrelitz, Germany, on February 6, 1919.

I.R.H.

Appendix A

REGARDING ERNST ROSENHAINER
FROM THE ROSTER

4/1/1910	Senior private
9/29/1910	Lance-corporal
4/12/1911	Lance-sergeant-major
11/19/1912	Second lieutenant (Patent Z 11 z)
8/5/1914	Induction
8/8/1914	Sent to the front with the 7th Thuringian Infantry Regiment 96, 4th Company
3/16/1915	Wounded near Grabice (Poland)
6/3/1915	Transferred to the 1st Reserve Battalion I.R. 96, in Gera
9/10/1915	Transferred to I.R. 96, 3rd Company
7/5/1916	Transferred to 1st Reserve Battalion 96, Gera
8/21/1916	Transferred to Landwehr I.R. 32 (197th Infantry Division), 12th Company
8/27/1916	Promoted to company commander, 12th L.I.R., 32
4/15/1918	First lieutenant, Reserves (A.K.O. o. 4/28/1918)
2/6/1919	Discharged in Neustrelitz (Mecklenburg, Germany)

The Iron Cross 1st Class was first proposed by the division's regiment on 9/4/1918.

Appendix B

ACTIVE COMBAT

CAMPAIGN AGAINST FRANCE. Infantry Regiment No. 96
3rd Army under General Baron Max Von Hausen.

8/20–24, 1914	Conquest of Namur
8/21, 1914	Château d'Arville
8/23, 1914	Namur

CAMPAIGN AGAINST RUSSIA 1914. 8th Army (East)

9/7–15, 1914	Battle near the Masurian Lakes & Pursuit Combat
9/8, 1914	Schätzelshöfchen (East-Prussia)
9/9, 1914	Henriettenfeld
9/10, 1914	Nordenburg-Ernstwalde
9/11, 1914	Kanzelberg
9/26, 1914	March into Southern Poland
9/28, 1914	Combat near Pinczow (Poland)
10/4, 1914	Combat near Opatow
10/22–28, 1914	Battles near the Rawka River
10/27, 1914	Combat near Strykow
11/14–16, 1914	Battle near Kutnow
11/14, 1914	Combat near Chelnino and Dabie
11/17–12/15, 1914	Battle near Lodz

11/18, 1914	Combat near Kolonie Juljanow
11/19, 1914	Combat near Wola Zytowka
In late November 1914:	Trench warfare near the Ner River (Babice-Lutomiersk)
12/2, 1914	Combat on Hill 181 near Lutomiersk
12/9–17, 1914	Battles near the Miazga River
12/18, 1914–7/2, 1915	Battles near the Rawka-Bzura River
12/19, 1914	Combat near Malgorzatow

January and February 1915, trench warfare near the Rylsk and the Rawka Rivers

Leopoldow—Rawa—Pockrzywna

3/5–6, 1915	Kawenczyn (1st/96, 1st and 2nd Company and 3rd/96)
3/10, 1915	Combat near Strzalki
3/16, 1915	Combat near Grabice (Wounded: Shot through left shin-bone)

FRANCE, 1916

10/2,1915–6/7, 1916	Battles between the Oise and Aisne Rivers
10/2,1915–5/7, 1916	Trench warfare near the Oise River
5/8–21, 1916	Battle on Hill 304 (Verdun)

CAMPAIGN AGAINST RUSSIA, 1916–1917

Combat activities by the L.I.R No. 32, 12th Company

8/31–9/6; 16, 17, and 9/23, 1916	Combat near Jaroslawice
10/14, '16–6/29, 1917	Trench Warfare K.& K. 2nd Army (East Galicia) (Imperial & Royal 2nd Army)
6/30–7/6, 1917	Defensive battle east of Zloczow
7/2 & 7/6, 1917	Combat near the Chorostowiec Forest
7/7–18, 1917	Trench warfare east of Zloczow
7/19–24, 1917	"Breakthrough" battle in East Galicia
7/23–24, 1917	Combat near Darachow
7/25–28, 1917	Pursuit battles in East Galicia

7/25 & 26, 1917	Combat near the Sereth River Crossing near Podhajczyki-Justynowce
7/29–8/2, 1917	Combat for the Ibrucz River Crossing between Zbruzc and Sereth
7/28–8/2, 1917	Combat near Husiatyn on the Zbrucz River
8/2–15, 1917	Trench warfare near the Zbrucz River
8/16–12/7, 1917	Trench warfare near the Sereth River

Lieutenant Rosenhainer was...

12/8, 1917–2/8, 1918	...in the battle zone near the Sereth River while hostilities were suspended and during the armistice.
2/9–23, 1918	...in the former battle zone of East Galicia after the peace agreement with the Ukraine. (The Ukraine had proclaimed its independence from Russia following the Bolshevic Revolution in November 1917.)
2/24–6/21, 1918	...Part of military operations in support of the Ukraine.
6/22, 1918–1/21, 1919	...with the occupation forces in the Ukraine.

Although my father refers to "Military Archives," he never explains where these may have been located. I believe that he may have found archival records either in Berlin, the capital of Germany, or in Gera, Thuringia, where he had received his military training before World War I. He does refer to the "Department of Defense" at the end of his page on "Military Decorations and Awards" (Appendix C).

I.R.H.

Appendix C

Auszeichnungen—Military Decorations and Awards

1. E. K. II (EISERNES KREUZ 2. Klasse): Iron Cross Second Class
   11/6/1914
2. REUSSISCHES EHRENKREUZ 3. Klasse mit Schwert:
   The Reuss Honor Cross Third Class with Swords   12/17/1914
3. MECKLENBURG-STRELITZER KRIEGSVERDIENSTKREUZ:
   The Mecklenburg-Strelitz Cross for Distinction in War with
   the inscription "Brave and True"   11/13/1915
4. MECKLENBURG-STRELITZER KREUZ FÜR AUSZEICHNUNG IM KRIEGE:
   Medal for Distinction in Action First Class, from the state of
   Mecklenburg-Strelitz   4/4/1918
5. VERWUNDETENABZEICHEN, SCHWARZ:
   Wound-Badge, black   6/5/1918
6. E. K. I (EISERNES KREUZ 1. KLASSE):
   Iron Cross First Class   9/12/1921

(Was first proposed to receive the Iron Cross First Class, by the regiment of the division on 9/4/1918.)
(Reichswehrministerium. Heeresleitung. Personalamt)
        Nr. II 1201/8, 21 PA. (1.)
(Department of Defense. Army Command. Personnel Office.)

Appendix D

CONVERSION TABLE AND ORGANIZATION OF GERMAN INFANTRY UNITS

CONVERSION TABLE

Kilometers	Miles	Kilometers	Miles
1	.6	6	3.7
2	1.3	7	4.6
3	1.9	8	5.0
4	2.5	9	5.6
5	3.1	10	6.2

1 meter = 1,09 yards   1 km = 1,000 meters

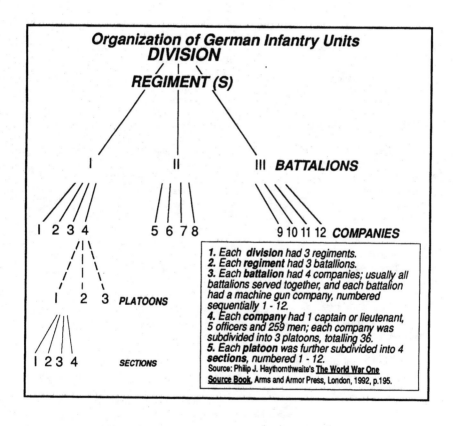

Organization of German Infantry Units
DIVISION
REGIMENT (S)

I   II   III *BATTALIONS*

I 2 3 4   5 6 7 8   9 10 11 12 *COMPANIES*

I   2   3   *PLATOONS*

I 2 3 4   *SECTIONS*

1. Each **division** had 3 regiments.
2. Each **regiment** had 3 batallions.
3. Each **battalion** had 4 companies; usually all
batallions served together, and each battalion
had a machine gun company, numbered
sequentially 1 - 12.
4. Each **company** had 1 captain or lieutenant,
5 officers and 259 men; each company was
subdivided into 3 platoons, totalling 36.
5. Each **platoon** was further subdivided into 4
sections, numbered 1 - 12.
Source: Philip J. Haythornthwaite's <u>The World War One</u>
<u>Source Book</u>, Arms and Armor Press, London, 1992, p.195.

Index

PLACES AND PERSONS

(First names were given where known. References to maps are printed in **boldface** type. Numbers in *italics* refer to the photographs.)

GENERAL

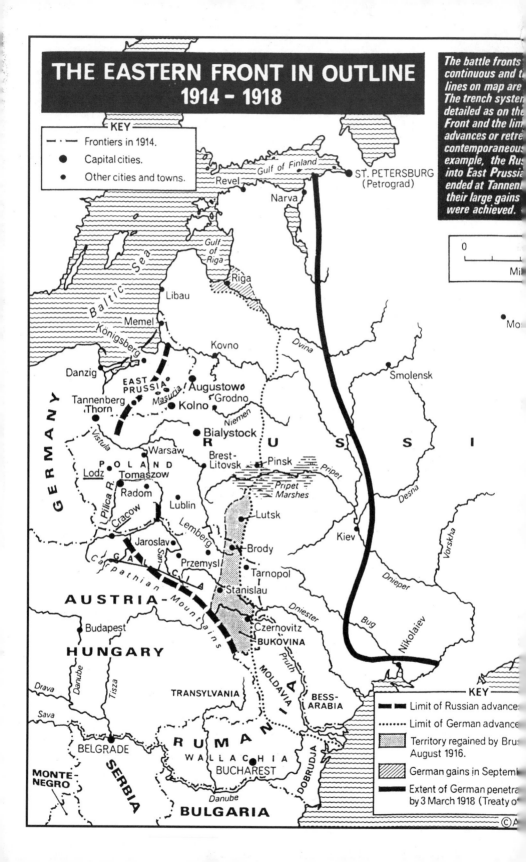

THE EASTERN FRONT IN OUTLINE
1914 – 1918

The battle fronts
continuous and t
lines on map are
The trench system
detailed as on the
Front and the lim
advances or retre
contemporaneous
example, the Rus
into East Prussia
ended at Tannenb
their large gains
were achieved.

KEY
- – · – Frontiers in 1914.
- ● Capital cities.
- • Other cities and towns.

0
Mi

Gulf of Finland
Revel
ST. PETERSBURG
(Petrograd)
Narva

Gulf
of
Riga
Riga
Libau
Baltic Sea
Dvina
Smolensk
Memel
Königsberg
Kovno
Danzig
EAST
PRUSSIA
Augustowo
Mo
Tannenberg
Thorn
Masuria
Kolno
Grodno
Niemen
GERMANY
Vistula
Bialystock
R   U   S   S   I
Warsaw
Brest-
Litovsk
Pinsk
Pripet
Lodz
POLAND
Tomaszow
Pripet
Marshes
Pilica R.
Radom
Lublin
Desna
Cracow
Lemberg
Lutsk
Vorskha
Jaroslav
Brody
Kiev
GALICIA
San R.
Przemysl
Tarnopol
Carpathian Mountains
Stanislau
Dnieper
AUSTRIA—
Dniester
Budapest
Czernovitz
Bug
Nikolaiev
HUNGARY
BUKOVINA
Drava
Danube
Tisza
MOLDAVIA
Sava
TRANSYLVANIA
BESS-
ARABIA
Pruth
A
BELGRADE
R   U   M   A   N   I   A
WALLACHIA
BUCHAREST
DOBRUDJA
MONTE-
NEGRO
SERBIA
Danube
BULGARIA

KEY
- ▬ ▬ ▬ Limit of Russian advance:
- ········· Limit of German advance
- ▨ Territory regained by Brus
  August 1916.
- ▤ German gains in Septemb
- ▬▬▬ Extent of German penetra
  by 3 March 1918 (Treaty of

©A